Modern Insurance Regulations and Its Supervision

Modern Insurance Regulations and Its Supervision

Dheeraj Razdan

CYBER TECH PUBLICATIONS
4264/3, Ansari Road, Daryaganj, New Delhi-110002 (India)
Ph.: 011-23244078, 011-43559448 Fax: 011-23280028
E-Mail: cyberpublicationsdelhi@yahoo.com
Website: www.cybertechpublications.com

MODERN INSURANCE REGULATIONS AND ITS SUPERVISION

Dheeraj Razdan

First Edition 2010

ıAsıan Offset Printers

Published by :

G.S. Rawat for **Cyber Tech Publications**
4264/3, Ansari Road, Daryaganj, New Delhi-110002 (India)
Ph.: 011-23244078, 011-43559448 Fax: 011-23280028
E-Mail: cyberpublicationsdelhi@yahoo.com
Website: www.cybertechpublications.com

Preface

This book refers to apparently universal accomplishments such as modern science and technology, democratic forms of government, urbanization, and so on.

On this account, modernity is opposed to tradition and replaces it everywhere with a rational "technoculture," rooted in the spread of a unique technological system.

If this is true, there is only one modernity and it is gradually erasing the cultural memory of humankind and homogenizing the globe. Insurance these days has become an indispensable part of human life because of the uncertainty of the things. In a way it is also a saving of the hard earned incomes of the people.

The purpose of the book is to make readers aware of the mechanism by which Insurance Companies do their business. This book presents everything about the theory and practice of the Insurance.

—*Author*

CONTENTS

1

BASIC INSURANCE REGULATIONS

INTRODUCTION

In many countries, including some industrial countries, effective insurance prudential regulation for the insurance industry has emerged only in the last two decades. In the past, some insurance supervisory approaches were based on the control of insurance products, pricing, and policy conditions as the basis for calculating the value of policyholder liabilities. Other supervisors used techniques based on solvency monitoring. During the 1990s, several supervisory authorities have increasingly adopted a market-based solvency monitoring approach, which appears to be gradually gaining universal acceptance. It is a great honour and pleasure for me to have been invited to speak at this biennial event – an event that has become a regular highlight in the calendar of banking supervisors from all over the world. And it is a particular pleasure to do so at a time when a major landmark in the long journey towards a safer and sounder global banking system has just been reached. I am of course referring to the new Basel capital adequacy framework. I have little doubt that, looking back, Basel II will be recognised as a critical milestone in our efforts to build a prudential framework that is strong, that works with market forces and that is sufficiently flexible to be adapted to country-specific circumstances as well as to the further evolution of the financial industry that no doubt is in store.

In my remarks today, however, I would like to cast my gaze more broadly and examine a number of implications of that never-ending evolution of the financial industry. In particular, I would like to explore with you the implications for the framework of prudential regulation and supervision of a deceptively simple word: "convergence". What I have in mind is the historically unprecedented process of convergence within the financial industry along three dimensions -- between financial institutions and capital markets; among different types of financial institutions; and among different national jurisdictions. My main focus will be on banking and insurance, where some of these forces have recently become more prominent, so that they pose major questions for those in charge of securing safety and soundness.

Convergence naturally implies shared interests and common challenges. In what follows, I will illustrate this obvious point in two ways. First, I will take a brief look back at how convergence has already shaped the parallel policy responses of banking and insurance supervisors. Then I will look forward and examine two emerging common challenges that will loom large in the coming years. One such challenge is to ensure that accounting standards and prudential frameworks are mutually consistent. This is necessary in order to achieve, simultaneously, the twin objectives of providing an accurate picture of the financial condition of a firm on the one hand, and of instilling the desired degree of prudence in its behaviour on the other. A second challenge is the need to strengthen the "macroprudential" or system-wide orientation of prudential frameworks, going from general principles – over which a growing consensus is forming – to practical day-to-day implementation. This is necessary to reinforce our safeguards against financial instability. In both of these areas, I will try to suggest ways in which we could make further progress.

A common thread in my remarks today is that the challenges posed by convergence highlight the importance of cross-fertilisation of different perspectives. In particular, there is much that banking and insurance authorities can learn from each other. And this dialogue should be embedded in a broader one encompassing other groupings too, notably accounting standard setters and central bankers. We are often tempted to highlight what makes us special rather than what we have in common. As a result, we can easily overlook those characteristics that bring us together and, in the process, fail to leverage our mutually reinforcing areas of expertise. We should build on these shared foundations to reach a common understanding of the problems and a common solution to them.

Insurance supervisors began working together at the broad international level less than a decade ago and are primarily concerned with policyholder protection rather than systemic risk or development issues.

This approach has strongly influenced the development of the internationally recognized regulatory principles. The underlying philosophy of modern insurance supervision is to identify problem companies early, act promptly, and apply effective intervention. This requires solvency margins, which are large enough to provide the time needed to resolve problems so that policyholder benefits are protected. Discussions are under way to set explicit international guidance on capital requirements.

Ireland (Insurance Corporation of Ireland-general) 1985

The Insurance Corporation of Ireland (ICI) came close to formal liquidation because of poor underwriting in its London branch and under reserving. Its parent at the time was Allied Irish Banks (AIB) and the failure of a major subsidiary could have caused a run. The Irish government purchased the company from the AIB and appointed an administrator.

Australia (HIH Insurance-general) 2001

HIH was a major liability underwriter in Australia. It collapsed in 2001 and an administrator was appointed. HIH was a major insurer of builders' liability and its demise disrupted conditions in the already weak construction sector. The failure of HIH also disturbed a number of other sectors, especially those which depend on professional indemnity insurance.

Korea (Insurance savings products) 1998-2001

Korean life and general insurers were encouraged to sell short-term savings products, some of which had deposit characteristics. Competition from banks and trust companies led to an interest rate war at a time of neutral or negative cash flows and massive deficits began to emerge. To prevent a run, the government guaranteed insurance liabilities. Much of the industry has since had to be wound up, or recapitalized by the government and sold.

Jamaica (Life insurance sector-savings products) 1996

The Jamaican life insurance industry had significant equity and fund flow cross-linkages with the banking sector, and was in some cases selling deposit equivalents as well as taking on major property exposures. A weak banking sector thus became exposed to an insolvent insurance industry and a rare case of insurance/banking contagion emerged. The government set up an asset management company, which has issued paper to fill balance sheet gaps.

While the insurance industry is changing in response to the demand for new products and services, the management and control of the insurers have not necessarily evolved as rapidly. As a result, there continues to be a wide range of practices in use for measuring and managing the risks in life and general insurance. In addition, there is continuing discussion between the industry and the supervisors about how the recent changes should translate into new practices and standards within the industry.

Capital, Accounting, and Actuarial Practices

At present, there is no equivalent to the Basel Capital Accord in the insurance sector. This is mainly due to the complexity in developing common standards that deal with the variety of insurance liabilities and asset combinations available. Accounting standards for insurance firms can vary markedly both in terms of the treatment of accruals and the rigor between (and within) countries. In addition, there is as yet no international actuarial standard for valuing policyholder-related liabilities, which is the single most important item in an insurer's balance sheet.

The differences in accounting and actuarial practices constitute a fundamental challenge for the work necessary to harmonize financial reporting standards that recognize the unique features of insurance, while meeting the needs of capital market participants and insurance supervisors alike. Insurance differs from banking in that the major liabilities do not emerge from a deposit or debt ledger; instead, they have to be estimated using actuarial or other techniques.

*Actuaries have developed measurement techniques to value policyholders and other liabilities. However, more work needs to be done to establish common international standards and to ensure that all aspects of the insurance business are covered. This work has to recognize the diverse nature of the insurance products and services that are offered. In some general insurance cases, the uncertainty attached to the liabilities can be considerably greater than that arising from the assets side of the balance sheet.**

The IAIS has issued draft general principles for consultation with its members on Capital Adequacy and Solvency (expected to be adopted in September 2001). However, these still do not specify qualitative requirements. They do recognize that the issue is complex and requires harmonization of international accounting, actuarial, and capital standards.

Reinsurance is a significant part of both life and general insurance. An important aspect of general insurance is the extent and the global nature of reinsurance. At best, reinsurance is only lightly regulated in most countries but represents one of the major assets on the balance sheets of many general insurers. The global general insurance industry remains heavily exposed to a small number of internationally active reinsurance companies based in Bermuda, Germany, Japan, Switzerland, United Kingdom, and the United States. Most have traditionally maintained very conservative accounts. However, capital market pressures for more 'efficient' use of capital, including a growing demand for transparency, tends to reduce capital ratios within these companies which could be having a negative effect on the overall security of the insurance sector.

The regulation of these institutions remains a controversial issue among insurance supervisors and the IAIS is working to develop standards in this area by 2002. While there is an agreement that the reinsurance arrangements that direct-writing companies have in place should be subject to supervision, there is disagreement on the extent to which the reinsurance companies should be supervised. However, even in countries where reinsurance firms are actively supervised, the focus is on contractual and prudential issues and the industry generally deals with the market conduct aspects of reinsurance.

IAIS AND THE ICP

The IAIS was established in 1994, some two decades after its banking and securities equivalents, and became a standard-setting body in 1996. The latest version of the ICP and the Insurance Core Principles Assessment Methodology (Methodology) was adopted by the IAIS members in October 2000.

The ICP provides a framework of 17 supervisory principles that need to be in place for effective insurance supervision. The IAIS regards these principles as essential supervisory and regulatory principles that all countries should implement. These include: governance issues, prudential requirements, information exchange, and sanctions (see Appendix I). A number of supporting documents (IAIS standards) have also been subsequently developed (licensing, on-site inspections, and derivatives), and new standards continue to be developed (reinsurance, solvency margin requirements).

The ICP Methodology strengthens the framework established by the ICP document in several ways. It provides an explanation of each principle in terms of its purpose and the elements that need to be reflected in the implementation. It prescribes a scheme for assessing the effectiveness of the insurance supervisory regime by prescribing over 200 assessments "criteria" comprising elements based on sound supervisory and regulatory practices. The IAIS also has recognized that assessments initiated by the Bank and the Fund "provided an opportunity to test both the applicability, clarity, and completeness of the ICP, as well as the degree to which an outside assessor could form an opinion regarding observance of the principles."

ICP ASSESSMENT PROCESS AND FINDINGS

Assessment Process

The assessment of the insurance supervisory system under the FSAP aims at: (1) identifying gaps in insurance sector regulation and supervisory practices; and (2) providing input for the overall stability assessment of the financial system. The main instrument used to achieve these objectives is an assessment of ICP observance (the ICP was issued by the IAIS in 1997 and revised in 2000). This is combined with the risk analysis of the broader financial system to establish vulnerabilities of the insurance sector.

Of the 20 ICP assessments completed so far under the FSAP, three of the early assessments were done using the 1997 version of the IAIS insurance supervisory principles, while the rest were based on the expanded version of these principles published in 2000. Thirteen ICP assessments have used the Methodology as a tool in the assessment, whereas the other seven were completed prior to its development. The countries assessed included five advanced, seven developing, and eight transitional countries; the insurance sectors in these countries are at various stages of development. While the small size of the sample precludes the drawing of any definitive conclusions, useful observations have been possible on the insurance supervisory vulnerabilities, their potential impact on financial stability, and in identifying development needs of the insurance system.

A range of tools was used in undertaking the assessments, the most important being the Methodology. The Methodology requires an assessment of supervisory processes not to be done in isolation, but after taking into account the risks and vulnerabilities from macroeconomic developments facing the insurance sector.

Active use is also made of any self-assessments done by supervisory authorities prior to the FSAP, relevant laws and regulations, interviews and discussions with supervisory authorities, other domestic regulatory bodies, groupings of actuaries, accountants, and auditors, and licensed insurance firms. To establish cross-sectoral linkages and form a view on overlapping issues, the assessors also discuss their findings with the banking and securities regulators.

Thus far, assessments have mainly involved staff from the Bank, supported by the Fund staff. Assessors have also been drawn from the Cooperating Official Institutions and, in some cases, after consultation with the IAIS. All assessments have mainly been carried out by at least one experienced insurance supervisor.

However, in the recent period, use is being made of two assessors where so dictated by country-specific factors such as the size of the insurance sector, the presence of complex financial institutions, or where development needs are great.

The assessors have adapted the application of the ICP to the stage of development of the insurance system. They have recognized that supervisory processes in different countries often reflect the local culture and attitude toward insurance, as well as the national authorities' ability to rely on the work of insurance accountants, auditors, and actuaries. In some cases, therefore, the assessors have modified the minimum set by the Methodology and assessed the country against the standard that the assessor felt the country should achieve. In many cases, they interpreted the ICP in slightly different ways, especially while assessing the principles relating to *Changes in Control, Liabilities, Sanctions, and Cross-Border Business*. This assessment calibration appears necessary given the differences in the systemic significance of the insurance system. Differing interpretations should, however, get minimized as the IAIS progressively sets supervisory standards underlying the ICP.

Assessors are strengthening the macroprudential analysis underlying the supervisory framework. Recent assessments have begun making systematic use of insurance-related financial soundness indicators to assist in the analysis of the insurance supervisory vulnerabilities. These include: ratio of the liabilities of life insurance companies to total bank deposits; ratio of the government bonds held by the insurance industry to the outstanding domestic debt; and ratio of total insurance premiums to GDP.

The Methodology identifies a set of preconditions for effective insurance supervision. These include: a sound legal and accounting system; procedures for resolving problems in insurance companies; effective market discipline; and sound and sustainable macroeconomic policies. There is, however, no explicit supervisory principle in the ICP document relating to the overall framework of insurance supervision.

Noting, however, that shortcomings in the overall conditions of insurance supervision may significantly impair the ability of the insurance supervisor to implement the principles, the Methodology requires assessors to evaluate the degree to which the identified preconditions are met and indicate potential problems stemming from any shortcomings. The Methodology, however, does not prescribe a basis to evaluate these preconditions. This remains a major limitation of the ICP and the Methodology, particularly as these preconditions cover issues that are generally outside of the control of the supervisor (operational independence, political interference, legal protection for supervisors). Future assessments should consider actions that supervisors can take to mitigate the effect of the preconditions that are not fully satisfied.

Assessments of the preconditions for effective insurance supervision reveal that some countries partially met the preconditions for effective insurance supervision, with qualifications related to the fact that while good laws were either in the process of being adopted or recently passed, they have not been tested in practice, or that the familiarity with the laws was weak. In some countries, assessors concluded that the judiciary system was weak, laws were outdated, and there were few qualified professionals (i.e., actuaries, accountants, auditors, and financial analysts). In a few cases, while the laws were outdated, the judiciary system was found to be satisfactory and some qualified professionals were present.

ASSESSMENT OF THE ICP

Main findings

Supervisory areas in which country practices were assessed to be generally satisfactory with respect to the ICP are: *Financial Reporting; Cross-Border Business Operations; Capital Adequacy and Solvency; Sanctions; Prudential Rules—Liabilities; and, Confidentiality*. The most commonly identified strengths were:

- *Financial Reporting*: Financial reporting requirements are set within the country and companies were required to file financial reports with the supervisory authority at least quarterly; audited financial reports were required annually.
- *Cross-Border Business Operations*: All foreign companies are required to be licensed to sell insurance in the country.
- *Capital Adequacy and Solvency*: Supervisory authority is able to prescribe capital and solvency standards that companies are required to meet.
- *Sanctions*: Many supervisory authorities have broad powers and a wide range of sanctions ranging from fines to licensing restrictions and de-licensing. Supervisors,

however, often have limited discretionary powers and can only apply sanctions in the event that the company violates the law.

- *Prudential Rules—Liabilities*: Supervisory authorities can set the basis for the valuation of liabilities. This is done either directly by the supervisory authority, through another branch of government, or through a domestic actuarial standard-setting body.
- *Confidentiality*: Staff of the supervisory authority is subject to professional secrecy requirements, and required to maintain the confidentiality of supervisory information.

It may be noted though that the satisfactory assessment of the supervisory practices relating to *liabilities* was mainly due to the fairly accommodating wording of the ICP. The formulation is broad enough to capture a wide range of established practices. To observe the principle, a supervisory authority must have powers to set the method and basis for the valuation of policy and other liabilities. However, the principle does not require that the authority be applied to any particular prudential standard. This is an important area that requires more work.

Areas in which supervisory practices were identified as weak include: *Organization of an Insurance Supervisor; Changes in Control; Corporate Governance; Internal Controls; Prudential Rules-Assets; Reinsurance; Market Conduct; and Derivatives and Off-Balance Sheet Items.* The most frequently cited shortcomings in the implementation of the principles in these supervisory areas were:

- *Organization of an Insurance Supervisor*: Weak institutional capacity characterized by inadequate supervisory skills and staff numbers, lack of financial resources and operational independence, and a nontransparent accountability framework.
- *Changes in Control*: The supervisor is often notified in advance but: there are no clear criteria for denying a

change in control; supervisory approval is not required; or the supervisor has no authority to deny a change in control. In some cases, the supervisor is not notified in advance of a change in control.

- *Corporate Governance and Internal Controls*: Lack of a description of the role and responsibilities of the board of directors of insurance companies in relevant legislation and regulations; and supervisors do not have the authority to define the role of directors. The most commonly identified reasons for non-observance or less than full observance of the principle on internal controls were the need to establish or strengthen risk management, asset-liability matching, and the supervisors' lack of authority to enforce an internal control regime in companies.
- *Prudential Rules—Assets*: Need to strengthen the investment rules and exposure limits for assets. In a few cases, the concern was that the investment rules were too limiting for reinsurance companies, which constrained the development of the market.
- *Reinsurance*: In all but one case, the identified shortcomings relate to the inadequacy of the supervisors' power to review or set standards for the use of reinsurance by direct-writing companies. In some instances, the assessor was also concerned that the supervisory authority needed greater power in setting retention limits (that is, a limit on the insurance risks that the direct-writing company would keep before seeking reinsurance protection).
- *Derivatives and 'Off-Balance Sheet' Items*: Need to define or strengthen the rules for the use of derivatives and the disclosures made by insurance companies in respect of their use of these instruments.
- *Market Conduct*: Need to ensure that insurance companies establish a complaint-handling system and supervisors need to have their role clarified and strengthened in this area.

Stage of Development of Insurance Sector

The stage of development of the insurance sector in the countries that were assessed varied substantially. Shortcomings in the observance of ICP in countries in which insurance plays a bigger role in the financial system can have a far greater impact on financial stability than in countries in which it is underdeveloped. Furthermore, supervisors in these two groups of countries face quite different challenges in exercising their responsibilities.

To gauge the impact of the stage of development of the insurance sector on ICP assessment findings, countries were grouped according to their relative standing on insurance penetration. Insurance penetration is used as a proxy for the stage of development of the insurance industry in a country relative to the global trends in the insurance business.

The results indicate that the degree of observance of ICP in countries with the most developed insurance sectors was significantly higher than that in countries with least developed insurance sectors.

The degree of observance of ICP in countries in different intermediate stages of development of the insurance industry is quite similar, but significantly lower than that of countries with the more developed insurance sectors. The incidence of non-observance of ICP in the areas of *Corporate Governance, Prudential Rules—Assets, Reinsurance, Internal Controls, Derivatives and 'Off-Balance Sheet' Items, Market Conduct,* and *Changes in Control* in countries that fall in the fourth quartile of the world distribution of insurance penetration was much more frequent than in countries with more developed insurance sectors.

Use of the Methodology

The use of the Methodology from May 2000 as the main tool for conducting the ICP assessments has had a significant impact on the assessment process. Comparison of the distribution of assessment grades in ICP assessments conducted with and without the use of the Methodology shows that its adoption has resulted in a more systematic approach and uniformity in the assessment of the countries' supervisory practices.

The major benefit from the Methodology has occurred in determining supervisory vulnerabilities relating to *Licensing, Corporate Governance, Organization of an Insurance Supervisor, and Capital Adequacy and Solvency*.

Observance of ICP and Transparency Practices of Insurance Supervisors

In conjunction with the ICP assessment, assessments are also being made of the transparency practices of the insurance supervisor. The assessment is undertaken with reference to the *IMF's Code of Good Practices on Transparency in Monetary and Financial Policies (MFP Transparency Code)*. A high degree of observance of ICP is associated with the high degree of observance of the MFP Transparency Code in the area of insurance and supervision and vice-versa.

Transparency practices of insurance supervisors are strongest in the area of public availability of information on financial policies, whereas transparency practices related to assurances of integrity of the insurance supervisor are most deficient. The most commonly identified shortcomings include: internal governance procedures are not publicly disclosed; cooperation and information-sharing agreements with other supervisory agencies are not transparent; publication of audited financial statements of the insurance supervisor is not done on a preannounced schedule; some of the procedures for appointment, terms of office, and removal of insurance supervisory officials are not publicly disclosed.

ICP Assessments and the IAIS Self-assessments

The IAIS initiated a self-assessment program based on the Methodology in October 2000. By the end of May 2001, nearly 61 percent of the members had responded. Ten of the twenty countries that underwent ICP assessment under the FSAP agreed to have the IAIS share their self-assessments with the

Bank and the Fund. The analysis of the differences in the assessment of observance of ICP between the ICP assessments and the IAIS self-assessments highlights some interesting patterns of how insurance supervisors assess their performance relative to peer assessments.

On average, five of the seventeen core principles were assessed differently between the ICP assessments and the IAIS self-assessments. In about 60 percent of the cases in which differences arose, countries assessed their insurance supervisory practices higher than the FSAP assessor, while in the rest the opposite was true. Four countries contributed disproportionally to the total number of differences in assessments. ICP assessments under the FSAP carried out in the absence of the use of the Methodology tended to assess countries' supervisory practices more flexibly in almost all areas. A possible explanation for the relatively large number of cases, in which countries assessed their observance of core principles more conservatively than the FSAP assessors, is that all IAIS self-assessments were based on the Methodology, whereas some ICP assessments were not. Supervisory areas, in which countries' practices were most often assessed better in the self-assessments were: *Licensing; Prudential Rules-Assets; On-Site Inspection;* and *Sanctions*. Conversely, country practices in the areas of *Derivatives and 'Off-Balance Sheet' Items; Reinsurance*; and *Corporate Governance* were most often assessed more conservatively in the IAIS self-assessments.

Overall, compared to the ICP assessments, the IAIS self-assessments have tended to focus more on formal observance with legislation and regulations and less on shortcomings in the enforcement of the existing supervisory framework. The emphasis is primarily from the point of view of the insurance supervisor rather than the insurance system as a whole so as to bring out issues relating to the operational independence of the insurance supervisor, or the extent of political interference that may be hampering the objectivity of insurance supervision. Another important aspect relates to the emphasis given under the FSAP in evaluating the supervisory regime within the context of the industry structure and the extent to which observance is adequate to address the emerging risks in the financial system.

Implications for Financial Sector Vulnerabilities

The ICP assessments are being used by the Fund staff as input into the stability assessments and by the Bank staff in the assessment of the overall development needs of the financial system. The assessment findings reveal several potential sources of supervisory risks and vulnerabilities. Two issues affecting stability have emerged. First, several assessments noted the stability risks emanating from weakness in the supervisory coordination among insurance, banking, and securities supervisors. While this was mainly in the case of countries where financial conglomerates exist or are gaining importance, the findings have a general application.

The insurance supervisor needs to monitor, along with other sector supervisors, the systems for risk identification and risk management across financial groups. A second area relates to strengthening the regulations relating to the prudential framework and its enforcement. These relate particularly to liabilities, where weak supervisory practices and requirements could conceal institutional weakness. In several cases, the ICP assessments cited the interconnectedness of financial institutions (insurance companies and banks) as having the potential to lead to a systemic problem. In one case, the issue highlighted was the failure of the supervisor to sign MOUs with foreign supervisors, given that most of the insurance companies were owned by foreign companies.

In a few cases, the assessments did not raise any stability-related concerns despite the countries' low level of observance of the ICP. This was due to the small size of the insurance sector relative to the other constituents of the financial system. In a few instances, the framework provided by the ICP was found inadequate in assessing the financial system, which was characterized by financial conglomerates and complex financial structures. In some cases, it became clear that the supervisory authority was not yet ready for a full ICP assessment under the FSAP and that a more comprehensive assessment of the preconditions of insurance supervision would have been more effective.

ICP ASSESSMENT RECOMMENDATIONS

Each ICP assessment identifies areas in which the supervisory authority should make changes to strengthen insurance supervision. ICP assessment recommendations have two objectives: (1) to strengthen supervisory practices where weaknesses are identified; and (2) raise the quality of insurance supervision in areas where, even though countries met the requirements of the ICP, additional steps could further foster the development of a sound insurance sector.

An analysis of the supervisory areas where recommendations were most frequently made was undertaken by groups of countries based on the stage of development of their insurance sectors. The patterns in the clustering of recommendations by broad areas of supervision support the view that assessors have addressed both objectives of this part of the assessment process. There is a clustering of recommendations in supervisory areas that were identified as weak in a significant number of countries.

Several recommendations were also made to strengthen the preconditions. These included the need to strengthen the legal infrastructure, supervisory resources, accounting, and disclosure practices. In addition, recommendations were also made in areas where observance of the ICP was assessed to be satisfactory but scope existed for further development.

While some of these recommendations address shortcomings in observance of the ICP, others attempt to raise the quality of insurance supervision above the prescribed minimum. The most commonly made recommendations related to *Organization of an Insurance Supervisor, Licensing, Prudential Rules, and Corporate Governance*:

- *Organization of an Insurance Supervisor*: Increase the number of staff in the authority; improve the quality of staff (training and recruiting) and the supervisory framework; enhance the independence of the supervisor; strengthen indemnity of the supervisory staff.

- *Licensing*: Increase the supervisor's authority and role; strengthen licensing criteria; tighten up the rules on composite companies; set rules for changes in control to be similar to licensing requirements.
- *Prudential Rules*: Strengthen investment rules and limits; upgrade rules for valuation of liabilities; strengthen capital requirements; define rules for the use and disclosure of derivatives; enhance supervision of reinsurance arrangements.
- *Corporate Governance*: Clarify or define what is expected of boards of directors; establish risk management practices.

FOLLOW-UP ON THE ICP ASSESSMENTS

National Authorities' Views on ICP Assessments

The degree to which the assessment process has the support from each country and the extent to which the national authorities are willing to take corrective action is an important part of the FSAP process. Feedback from national authorities shows that the assessment process was found to be useful in the implementation of the ICP. The assessments have provided impetus and direction to national authorities' ongoing efforts to bring their insurance legislation and regulatory framework in observance with internationally accepted supervisory practices. Several countries report difficulties in the implementation of the principle relating to Corporate Governance. This is mainly due to the lack of development in the local standards of general business practice or legislation. The "Fit and Proper" test and "Coordination and Cooperation with Other Supervisors" are also mentioned as being difficult to implement by a number of countries. In addition, some countries reported resistance on the part of the insurance industry to changes in regulations introduced as a consequence of the recommendations based on the ICP assessment.

Technical Assistance

Usually, the assessments list recommended actions that should be assigned priority from the perspective of addressing short-term vulnerabilities or reform required to strengthen the overall supervisory framework. These have provided a good basis for independent follow-up by the supervisory authority or by requesting follow-up technical assistance from the Bank and the Fund. In several cases, the countries have reported that the recommendations helped them to formulate their own policy priorities. In three of the twenty cases assessed so far, follow-up technical assistance has been provided. These have been in the areas of insurance legislation, regulation, and organization of the insurance supervisory body.

The Bank and Fund staff have also received from the IAIS a request for technical assistance identified by the supervisory authorities as follow-up to the IAIS self-assessments completed recently. These have been in the areas of insurance legislation, setting up the insurance supervisory agency, corporate governance, and prudential regulations. The Bank and Fund staff are in dialogue with the IAIS on the scope and modalities of such technical assistance and ways in which it can be integrated with the pre- and post-FSAP work.

CONCLUDING OBSERVATIONS

The FSAP provides the ICP assessments a useful context for assessing stability and development needs of the insurance system. The macroeconomic and financial vulnerabilities, coupled with a complete assessment of the bank and securities market supervision, allow the insurance sector findings to be placed in perspective. Some further analytical work is, however, required with respect to how insurance enhances financial system efficiency and affects financial stability. Further, while the Methodology should remain the main tool for assessing insurance supervisory systems, the assessors need to supplement it with other IAIS standards and guidance while evaluating risks and vulnerabilities specific to individual jurisdictions. This is especially important while conducting assessments in more complex insurance markets, given the gaps and the need for further improvements in the ICP and the Methodology.

Preconditions Assessment

Assessment of the preconditions is a critical element of the assessment process. However, the criteria for assessing the preconditions for effective insurance supervision need urgent attention.

The assessment experience reveals that in cases where significant shortcomings in the preconditions for effective insurance supervision are identified, the focus of the FSAP review could be better directed at reviewing ways to strengthen observance with the preconditions. This would assist the assessment process in focusing in on the key issues that would strengthen the insurance supervisory system.

Areas for Improving the ICP and the Methodology

The use of the ICP as a tool in the FSAP needs to be enhanced in several areas. While the ICP sets out the powers and responsibilities that insurance supervisors should have, they do not specifically require that supervisors implement and use these supervisory powers. Some of the principles cover a broad topic while others deal with a narrow issue. The principles dealing with prudential issues (assets, liabilities, capital and solvency, and reinsurance) need to be developed further.

Three broad areas in which the IAIS could therefore initiate work to improve the ICP are: increase the scope of the ICP (market conduct); improve the clarity of the ICP (organization, licensing, cross-border operations); and remove overlapping criteria (confidentiality).

Critical to the success in developing and defining sound international standards in these areas is the work that is under way with the International Accounting Standards Board and the International Actuarial Association. As such, these standard-setting bodies should be encouraged to continue to place importance to their work in setting international standards for insurance enterprises.

Linkages to Stability

In considering the assessment findings and the relationship between the observance with the ICP and financial stability, it became clear that more experience and a well-defined macroprudential framework relevant for the insurance sector is necessary in order to make a determination of the important linkages. However, the assessments clearly show that the risks to insurance stability is greater in situations in which the preconditions for effective insurance supervision are not fully met and there is less than full observance with the prudential principles. This, together with a high insurance penetration ratio, could indicate an important supervisory vulnerability. In addition, in the course of carrying out the FSAPs, a number of potential systemic issues have been identified, some of which have quite subtle operational modalities. The issue of financial stability and systemic risk will gain prominence during the ICP assessments of more complex insurance markets. It also points to the need for further improvements in the ICP and the development of a taxonomy of systemic exposures in the nonbank financial sector.

Insurance is the study of risk financing through risk pooling. In a dynamic economy like the one we have in Hong Kong, a myriad of things can go wrong everyday with our life, our health, our home, our car, and our business. The use of insurance to reduce the adverse financial impact in case of a loss has become an important element of financial planning in our society.

Risk management, as a building block of financial planning, seeks to identify the risks a person or a business faces and evaluating their financial impacts in case of occurrence. Once the relevant risks have been identified, the risk manager must determine the need for insurance based on his financial goal and assess the various risk handling tools available to him in order to select the one that can best serve his financial goal.

In order to make a sound risk management decision, the risk manager must have a thorough understanding of the designs and functions of various insurance products available for loss reduction and the new products and future trends of development in insurance.

This course deals with the analysis of financial and business exposures to loss and risk management techniques, the risk meeting alternatives and their economic, legal, and social implications, and the role of insurance in risk management. The proper functioning of insurance relies heavily on the validity of the legal contract between the insured and the insurer. This course will also explain the characteristics of the contractual agreements pertaining to each type of insurance product. Moreover, it will explain to students the major theories underlying each type of product that are essential for the risk manager to effectively conduct the cost and benefit analysis on the risk managment program.

For example, how are premiums for life insurance policies determined and how do we compare the costs of different policies that are compatible with our need? In addition to the analysis of insurance from the consumer's perspective, this course will also explain to students the structure of the insurance industry and its impact on the pricing of insurance products. The operation of insurance companies and the need for government regulations on the industry that are necessary for maintaining insurance as a viable tool for risk management will also be discussed.

EXTENDING THE THEORY TO MEET THE PRACTICE OF INSURANCE

Formal insurance arrangements date back at least to ancient Greece. Marine loans in that era advanced money on a ship or cargo. It would be repaid with substantial interest if the voyaged succeeded, but forfeited if the ship was lost, much like the structure of contemporary catastrophe bonds. The interest rate covered both the cost of capital and risk of loss.

Direct insurance of sea risks, using premiums, probably started around 1300 in Belgium. The first known life insurance policy was written in 1583. By the end of the 17 th century, sea risk insurance had evolved to a competitive process between underwriters evaluating risks and meeting at Lloyd's coffee house, the precursor to Lloyds of London.

Today, insurance is a major industry established throughout the world. It moves progressively into new fields. For example, health insurance was virtually unknown in the United States prior to 1929 and now pays for more than 10 percent of the US GDP. Risks ranging from a Camcorder breaking down to being sued for sexual harassment are all insurable events. In recent decades, economic attention has caught up with the remarkable burgeoning of the insurance industry. This is largely attributable to the explosion in attention to information in economics. Indeed, insurance so well fits this attention that it is a major topic of introductory discussions about the role of information in economics. Moreover, the core insurance topics of moral hazard and adverse selection have been transplanted to fields like labor economics and finance.

This sounds like a happy confluence of theory and practice growing up alongside one another: theory improves by studying practice, and practice draws on the results of theory. A principal theme of this essay is that perception is fundamentally wrong. We believe that there is an increasing divergence between the theory of insurance and insurance practice. Consider the following quiz about optimal insurance.

1. Suppose that a risk goes from negligible to possible--for example, the increased probability of a terrorist accident on US soil after September 11, 2001. Would you expect the private market to provide (a) more insurance; or (b) less insurance?
2. A 70 year-old unmarried woman has three children, all of whom are comfortably middle class. Would you expect her to be more likely to hold (a) an annuity; or (b) life insurance?
3. A consumer buys a $620 camcorder and is offered insurance in case it breaks. The insurance is for three years and costs $120, supplementing the 1 year parts and labor that comes with the camcorder. The probability of a camcorder needing a repair over three years is 8

percent (mostly in the first year), with average repair costs of $125. Would you expect the person to (a) decline the insurance; or (b) accept the insurance.

In each case, optimal insurance principles suggest that (a) is the right answer. But (b) is the answer we often see in the world. Coverage for terrorism risk plummeted after the attacks in September 2001, despite the greater demand for care. About seven times more elderly people have life insurance than annuities, in spite the fact that incomes of children are rising over time. And insurance against small cost consumer durables is among the most profitable items sold by commercial electronics stores. For almost all products, one in five of the customers purchase it; for some it is four in five. We argue in this paper that these examples are not minor anomalies, but reflect a systematic tendency for insurance in practice to differ from insurance in theory. We discuss and grade a number of insurance settings: mortality, health, and property risk for individuals; and property, liability, environmental, and terrorism risk for businesses. In the vast majority of cases, we argue that insurance in practice diverges from insurance in theory.

The divergence is of two forms. First, insurance is often purchased-sometimes at excessive prices--when theory would suggest it should not, and many significant risks that should be insured are not. The case of life insurance among the elderly, or insurance for minor consumer durables, is an example of the former. The lack of coverage for terrorism insurance is an example of the latter. Second, there are significant mismatches between parties who should bear risk and those who actually do. Risks can be borne by public entities, private (for profit and not-for-profit) firms, and through financial markets. In practice, the allocation of risk across these entities seems suboptimal. Governments insure risks that the private sector might better bear, and financial markets, with their vast resources and wide participation, are not the risk bearer for many large private risks.

The divergence between theory and practice is not a result of moral hazard or adverse selection. In many settings with failures, information is as close to symmetric as it is possible to be, and moral hazard is extremely implausible. Rather, we argue that the divergence of insurance theory and practice is a result of three phenomena, the first on the supply side, the second on the demand side, and the third a true joint product. The first is highly incomplete diversification on the part of insurers.

This outcome, we believe, arises due to contracting problems on the supply side of insurance. Investors in insurance companies may be nearly risk neutral for virtually all insurance decisions, but managers of insurance companies are not. Risks that are hard to predict, or are correlated across insureds, may result in the insurance company losing significant amounts of money, with some people being blamed and losing their jobs. We argue that this is an important reason why large but nontraditional risks, e.g., terrorism or long-term health care, are not insured.

Contracting difficulties also help explain why financial markets, with assets in the trillions, as opposed to billions for insurance companies, have not played a more significant role in insurance. One challenge is to secure collateral from investors-the ideal source to cover claims-in case a claim arises. Catastrophe bonds are a small step in this direction, but there is no reason to use as collateral only fixed-income investments.

In time, we expect, individuals will be able to participate in insurance pools by pledging such assets as stocks and real estate. A second challenge is to marry insurance expertise with ready pools of capital. Such marriages have been highly successful in such areas as venture capital and hedge funds.

The standard financial arrangement for such contracts (a management fee and a share of profits) may not be sufficient, though, since profits on insurance may be large until an adverse event occurs. Still, there is plenty of money to write insurance, and ample expertise to write the insurance effectively, even if bringing the two together will require innovative institutions and creative contracts.

The demand side contributes its share to the poor performance of insurance relative to theoretical par. The central problem is that people have severe difficulties making decisions where small probabilities and significant stakes are involved. These difficulties have been discussed in the burgeoning literature on behavioral economics and behavioral decision-making, which was pioneered by Amos Tversky and Daniel Kahneman, and for which Kahneman shared the 2002 Nobel Memorial Prize in Economics.

People seem (irrationally) fearful of uninsured losses. They overly project their unhappiness and regret were a bad event to occur, and they misjudge probabilities. As a result, people often insure when theory would say they shouldn't; they insure against small risks; they take deductibles that are way too small; and they insure against events that though tragic do not change the marginal utility of income.

The third problem is what we refer to as probability monopoly. It arises when sellers of insurance know risks much better than buyers, and when there is limited competition. Sellers then set prices well above actuarial and administrative cost so as to capitalize on potential buyers' misestimates. Buyers that overestimate the risk of breakdown purchase insurance, at a profit for the insurer.

In the remainder of the paper, we develop these themes about the operation of insurance markets in theory and practice. We introduce areas where we think the theory of insurance should be extended if it is to explain practice, such as understanding what benefits actual purchasers believe they get when they purchase insurance. We start with some basics on when we expect insurance to be widespread, and then turn to an evaluation of insurance markets in practice.

We note at the outset that this is a thought piece. Thus, it tries to present neither rigorous theory nor detailed empirical analysis. It draws data from many sources and arenas to illustrate its themes.

And it is speculative in part to be provocative. Thus, for example, we provide our own grades for the functioning of insurance markets across many areas.

INSURANCE IN THEORY

In many arenas insurance does work well. We begin by examining what we might think of as par performance for insurance markets, and then grade various insurance areas on how they do on these criteria.

The principal goal of insurance, as assessed by economists, is to transfer resources from low marginal utility of income states to those where the marginal utility of income is high. If insurance is actuarially fair, this process will continue until the marginal utility of money is constant across states. When unfair, insurance will be partial, and greater the greater is risk aversion.

Insurance is most effective when losses are common enough to be of concern but not frequent enough to be routine. Neither asteroid strikes nor car scratches make for good insurable events. Insurance for routine events requires repeated administrative expense that makes the insurance less valuable; the risk spreading benefits are also low.

Insuring extremely rare risks also involves reasonable expense, with little compensating gain. Similarly, transactions costs make it important that risks be relatively well defined, and assessable once they happen. Otherwise, claims assessment and litigation can be exceedingly expensive. For most familiar risks, e.g., a house burning down, we would think this condition would be met. However, the recent experience with the one-or-two incident World Trade Center catastrophe makes it clear that there are important exceptions, even with burning buildings. Such ambiguities are more likely where new classes of risk come into play.

Effective insurance also requires that unobservable actions, i.e., moral hazard, not be too significant. Fortunately, major aspects of non-monetary, uncovered loss often assure that this is the case. Thus, for example, rational drivers are not likely to drive at too high speeds because they are insured, and people are unlikely to smoke because they know that if they get cancer, they will receive treatment. The potential for death and disability in these cases counts at least as heavily as covered losses. Monitorable actions (e.g., determining whether a building is kept in safe condition), and risks due to an external source (e.g., earthquakes) also diminish the moral hazard problem.

These important attributes for effective coverage are generally associated with the demand for insurance. The supply side of insurance also determines significantly how well it works. Two critical questions are how diversifiable the risk is, and whether there is an entity that is capable of bearing it. Most familiar insured risks, e.g., the risk of death, are readily diversified cross-sectionally, since the experiences of members of large pools of insureds are effectively independent. There are, however, many critical risks-e.g., the costs of long-term care-where expected costs for different individuals are strongly correlated; they are so-called aggregate risks. Cross-sectional diversification is not possible with these risks, and other risk-sharing arrangements need to be made.

Concerns about the supply-side may seem misplaced in an industry like insurance, where there are many firms and barriers to entry seem relatively modest. Still, competition in insurance seems far from perfect. As one demonstration of this, consider a fundamental attribute of perfectly competitive markets: the law of one price. In a competitive market, the same good should sell at the same price everywhere.

Medigap is an interesting market to study because the policies that can be offered are absolutely standardized, being set by law. Thus, there are no hidden provisions to account for. Still, the price for insurance varies by a factor of four across companies.

AARP has a uniform price by age, while none of the other insurers do. In a situation where consumer shopped around regularly, this would not occur.

Even businesses find it hard, or seem reluctant, to shop for the best insurance deal. Warren Buffett, one of America's shrewder insurance purveyors, announces periodically in his Berkshire-Hathaway report that he will not be writing various types of business coverage this year because the rates are too low.

Buffett suggests that despite expected losses, his competitors are writing insurance to keep their old customers, expecting these customers to stick with them when prices rise.

His competitors at least think cross-elasticity of demand is low for insurance. We consider a large number of potential individual and business risks, and evaluate them on these criteria, effectively seeing how well they are likely to be spread.

Consumer Risks

We analyze three major consumer risks. The first is mortality. Though death is certain, its timing is not. Family-oriented breadwinners would like to insure against early departure. Thus, we expect term life insurance to be a common asset in non-retirement years. Once retired, the demand should tip to annuities that guard against outliving one's assets.

Mortality risk is a classic case where we expect insurance to perform well. On the individual side, the event is obviously infrequent, so that administrative costs are not too high. The loss is also well defined, and moral hazard is contained.

On the supply-side, it is relatively easy to diversify mortality risk across people, since aggregate death rates are generally fairly stable.

The second risk is to health-more specifically the danger of incurring conditions that are expensive to treat. We divide health risks into two categories. The first is short-term health risks. People have variable health needs in the current years, which conventional health insurance covers. Health risk is somewhat less conductive to insurance than is mortality risk. In part, the need for health care is less ideal. While some health needs are truly random, others are routine, such as an annual physical or well-baby care. The costs of running payments for such services through insurance may be high. In addition, moral hazard is an issue in health care. People may (or may not) take much worse care of themselves when they have health insurance-termed ex ante moral hazard-but they certainly use more care when insured than when uninsured (ex post moral hazard), e.g., come in for minor aches and pains. Health insurance is not run like a contingent claims market. Whatever your health condition, the more you spend, the greater the cost you impose on the insurer.

Some health risks are also long-term. Long-term care expenses provide a salient case. About one-third of the elderly will use nursing home care on a sustained basis, and this care can be expensive-costing upwards of $40,000 per year (National Center for Health Statistics, 2003). Because a lot of the gains from long-term care insurance involve pooling people who die without using a nursing home with those who do, this care needs to be purchased before significant morbidity sets.

Risk about future health type is related to long-term care risk. Health insurance for individuals, or the groups they purchase with, is usually experience rated. Should an individual's health decline, or the health of the average member of the group decline, the premium increases. Thus, one might expect people to want insurance against the risk of becoming high cost in the future (Pauly, Kunreuther, and Hirth, 1995; Cochrane, 1995; Cutler, 1996).

Adverse long-term health events are sufficiently infrequent, but not too much so, that insurance makes a good deal of sense, at least in theory. But these risks challenge conventional insurance in three other ways. As with short-term health insurance, moral hazard is likely to be an issue in long-term insurance: if insured, move grandma to the nursing home. In addition, the loss is poorly defined. When does a person need long-term care, and when is she capable of functioning on her own? What does the appearance of a health event today signal about potential future spending?

These information problems undermine the viability of long-term insurance. On the supply-side, there is a substantial concern about diversifying these risks. When future medical costs increase for some people-e.g., because expensive new medical technologies become available-they will increase for others as well. Similarly, if new medical knowledge extends survival at older ages, it will yield such benefits to millions. The unhappy side effect is that a much greater percentage of the population will spend a fair amount of time in nursing homes. Such properties of long-term health risks imply that cross-sectional diversification will not be entirely possible.

The final individual risk that we address is property and casualty risk. People own homes, cars, and consumer durables that may burn, crash or break. Consequently, they may want to insure them. Property and casualty insurance has many attributes that are favorable to insurance coverage. The major exception is moral hazard. One might imagine that people drive faster when they are insured, or take less good care of their house or other durables. Some evidence suggests that this is the case (see Cohen and Dehejia, 2003, for a summary), though the evidence is far weaker than for moral hazard in medical care utilization.

While mortality, health, and property/casualty risk are the major individual risks that we consider, it is important to note that there are other risks we are not discussing. Most people owe money on a house, and face a choice between an ostensibly risky debt payment (an adjustable-rate mortgage) versus a fixed, insured payment (a fixed rate mortgage). However, it is not obvious which form should be preferred, i.e., whether the borrower should protect the bank against interest rate movement, or vice versa. We might analyze this financial choice in the same way as other forms of insurance.

People might also like insurance for their human capital, for example to guard against depreciation of their skills-think travel agents--or prolonged unemployment. There is public insurance for some of these risks, via unemployment insurance, workers' compensation, and disability insurance. But many risks, e.g., lost productivity, are insured by no one. Moral hazard is clearly a substantial issue for many of these risks. In the interest of brevity, however, we do not consider the entire range of risks that individuals face.

Business Risks

Many business risks are similar to individual risks. Businesses own property, for example, and there is uncertainty associated with damage to that property. Businesses are also liable for damages if someone is injured on their premises, if they are found to cause health harms, or if their employees are mistreated. As with health risks for individuals, we divide property and casualty risks for businesses into two groups. Short-term risks are the most common type of business risk. They encompass most damage to property, and litigation exposure. Most of these risks involve relatively infrequent events (but not too infrequent) and generally have well-defined losses (the World Trade Center being a notable exception). There may be some moral hazard in these actions, but we suspect it is not too large.

Most, but not all, short-term business risks can be diversified cross-sectionally. The most prominent exception is terrorism risk, where the potential losses are so large that even having a substantial insurance pool does not drive the variability of losses particularly low. As a result, we note ease of diversification as being either favorable or adverse.

Long-term property and casualty risks are those risks that will not be realized for some time. Firms may discover only years later that the chemicals in their product increase cancer risk. In the same fashion, obstetricians may be sued years after a birth for complications that were only realized later. One can think of the liability revolution in the 1970s and 1980s as a bad realization of a long-tailed risk. Once again, this long-tailed risk makes diversification difficult, since new knowledge increasing claims against one business are often correlated with increases in claims against another. Difficulties with diversification are a major problem in many litigation risks.

Firms also face risk about employment decisions. Firms may be sued for sexual harassment, unjust dismissal, or unfair hiring practices. This risk has many of the attributes of long-term property and casualty risk. The event is not very frequent and is well-defined, but may not be diversifiable cross-sectionally.

The same legal changes that make liability for pollution or medical harms greater than are thought also increase the potential losses from employment issues.

Finally, businesses have risky obligations for the pensions and health care of retired workers. Many large firms have defined benefit pension plans-plans that obligate them to a specific payment based on the age of the retiree and number of years of service. Retiree health insurance payments may work the same way. If pension costs rise more rapidly than expected, or a firm's earnings fall substantially, the firm may be unable to meet its pension obligations. Moral hazard is of clear importance in this risk. Firms that are doing poorly will underfund their pensions, knowing that if the firm fails it will not have sufficient assets to pay out its pension liabilities.

Diversification issues are also important, since pension and health costs tend to rise jointly across firms. For this and other reasons (perhaps the political imperative of caring for penurious retirees), pension obligations are generally insured through the public rather than private sector. As with individuals, there are other financial risks that businesses might like to insure.

Using sophisticated financial instruments, businesses can often do this. Companies selling abroad can hedge exchange rate risk, and businesses can insure interest rate risk through appropriate derivative securities. To keep our analysis manageable, we avoid consideration of these financial risks.

Bundling Insurance and Other Services or Attributes

Many products that are officially sold or presented as insurance provide more than just financial protection; they bundle other services with the risk benefits. These additional benefits are important to account for in evaluating the insurance policy. In some arenas, insurance products have integrated backwards into purchasing services, or at least procuring them. This enables insurers to purchase products at substantially reduced rates. Health insurance is the most prominent example.

When insurance is coupled with provision, the combination may have significant advantages in exerting leverage as a buyer. This should not be thought of as exclusively or even predominantly as an insurance product, i.e., as a risk-spreading device. Many insurance products couple insurance with a tax shield.

The buildup in whole life insurance is not taxed, for example, making that product an excellent vehicle for saving. Health insurance that pays for routine care costs is also a tax dodge, saving the taxation that would be associated with wage and salary payments. The primary motivation for such policies is not the financial risk per se, but the combination of risk reduction and tax rewards.

Still other insurance programs, especially in the public sector, have a strong redistributional element. Government "insurance" programs, such as Social Security and unemployment insurance, almost always have an intended redistributional role. That is, judged ex ante, some participants are hurt and others helped. But even in the private sphere, we see redistribution at play.

Thus, young workers usually subsidize older workers in employer-provided health insurance. Alas, there is no way to discuss insurance without referring to instruments that work as buyers cooperatives, and insurance that significantly redistributes income. These instruments are not strictly insurance. This caveat should inform our discussion below.

INSURANCE IN PRACTICE-CONSUMER RISKS

In this section, we evaluate how insurance for consumer risks fare in practice. Because we consider a number of risks, our analysis is necessarily impressionistic. We rely on conclusions of detailed research studies where possible, and analysis of aggregate data in many cases. For many types of risk, we conclude that insurance performs substantially less well than is anticipated by theory.

Mortality

As Yaari (1965) first noted, life insurance and annuities cater to mutually exclusive circumstances-living too long and living too short; one would not expect the same person to want both in force at the same time.

In practice, life insurance is very common, and annuitization is very rare. The 2001 Survey of Consumer Finances estimates that two-thirds of families have life insurance, including as many as 90 percent of two-adult families. In total, families have $16 trillion of assets in life insurance (American Council of Life Insurers, 2003). Annuities, by contrast, are owned by only a small share of the population, usually as one option in a retirement plan, e.g., with an IRA rollover. Only 8 percent of the population aged 70 and older has an annuity, compared to 78 percent of that group that has life insurance (Brown, 1999). Annuity reserves total less than $2 trillion.

Without knowing individuals' preferences exactly, despite knowing their assets, earnings and family and health status, we cannot tell what insurance arrangement is optimal for them. A married worker might skip life insurance if he does not value highly the consumption of his non-working spouse. Similarly, a couple may not want an annuity in old age if it is penurious relative to assets, or can deal with a declining consumption stream. Still, one suspects that such cases are rare, and that large consumption changes individuals might experience due to lives cut short or stretched long are not intended. The research literature takes this perspective in evaluating the adequacy of annuitization and life insurance: it has examined whether these products are purchased in sufficient quantity to minimize consumption changes in the event that bad outcomes are realized. Because of the centrality of life insurance and annuities to debates about social security reform, their use has been considered in detail.

The spread of life insurance is expected and valuable, and important as a source of savings as well as security. Still, two aspects of life insurance have drawn attention as being sub-optimal. The first is the substantial rate of life insurance holdings among the elderly (see Brown, 1999, for a review). Some of the elderly, a group whose children are presumably independent, would rationally want life insurance protection (if pensions depend on the survival of one spouse, for example) but three-quarters is a very high share, and even many elderly without dependents have life insurance.

Some work has focused on the high rate of life insurance coverage among the elderly. One proposed explanation is that social security provides too much annuitization, and people offset that by purchasing life insurance. Brown (1999) finds evidence that this is not the case, however; term life insurance is not more likely to be held by people with larger social security payments. He suggests that other explanations are more important: tax policy that allows for tax-free buildup in whole life insurance or tax-free payment of burial costs; and inertia from purchasing life insurance earlier in life. The exact share attributable to each is not entirely known, but the non-tax explanations such as status quo bias (Samuelson and Zeckhauser, 1988) are surely important. The extent of life insurance during the working years seems broadly appropriate, though concerns linger. In particular, some authors have worried about whether people in their working years are sufficiently insured. Recent studies suggest that too few families have life insurance, and many families that have insurance are underinsured. Bernheim, Forni, Gokhale, and Kotlikoff (1999) use data on family income, assets, and demographic characteristics for people aged 51 to 61 (from the Health and Retirement Survey) to examine the consumption consequences should they die.

They estimate that 30 percent of wives, and 11 percent of husbands, would suffer a consumption decline of 20 percent or more if their spouse passed away, a large enough reduction to rule out the explanation of rational preferences, apart from the joint explanation of little concern for and insufficient bargaining power of the dependent spouse. The shortfall in insurance coverage is more surprising given government tax subsidy to employer-paid premiums, and to investment earnings during the life of a policy.

The extent of underinsurance varies with socioeconomic characteristics. After correcting for income and assets, underinsurance is more common among lower income families, and among couples with very asymmetric earnings (for example, one-earner couples). In the latter families, the death of the higher earning spouse would often pose severe hardships for the surviving spouse. Indeed, work by Bernheim, Carman, Gokhale, and Kotlikoff (2001) suggests that two-thirds of poverty among surviving women and one-third of poverty among surviving men results from a failure to purchase sufficient life insurance.

Adverse selection could explain the underpurchase of insurance among some families, but the literature does not suggest that this is important in life insurance. Cawley and Philipson (1999) document that prices decrease with additional purchases, where adverse selection would imply the reverse. They also find that individual forecasts of mortality probabilities do not help predict purchase of life insurance. Life insurance is also estimated to have very low administrative expense. More likely is that these families are simply not planning adequately for adverse events that may occur: they do not forecast the extent of consumption declines should death occur; life insurance never becomes a conscious decision the family makes; or the male decision-maker does not weigh the utility of his spouse very highly.

Annuitization. The central question about annuities is why so few people purchase them. As noted, less than 10 percent of people aged 70 and older have any private annuity, though essentially all elderly have social security and many elderly have defined benefit pension plans.

The administrative load in annuities provides a partial explanation. Mitchell, Poterba, Warshawsky, and Brown (1999) estimate that the load on annuities is about 15 to 20 percent. About half of that is a result of adverse selection; the remainder is marketing costs, processing costs, and insurer profit.

Still, it does not seem possible to explain the low rate of annuitization, even with these administrative costs. First, the investment returns in annuities are strongly tax favored. Second, risk spreading concerns make annuities worthwhile. In a utility-based simulation model of the annuitization decision, Mitchell et al. estimate that people should be willing to pay an administrative fee of 25 percent to annuitize their assets. That is far above the cost that we see in practice. Conceivably, strong bequest motives could explain low rates of purchase. But annuities would be one way to insure the size of the bequest. The literature has not explored the degree or nature of bequest motivation that could help explain these results. We expect that few could stand up to rational economic scrutiny.

The literature speculates more about 'behavioral' explanations for the low rate of annuitization. Anecdotal evidence suggests that many elderly may not be aware of or understand annuities, and many fewer have priced them (further undercutting the high administrative cost explanation for modest use). Other potential customers may fear paying money to an insurance company only to die shortly thereafter without much return. Along the latter lines is the seemingly inexplicable preference some people have for annuities that guarantee a payment for a certain number of years, even if the annuitant dies before that time.

SUMMARY

As a means of keeping track of the evidence, we provide our net assessment of the various insurance markets we consider. To keep the analysis simple, we use a three-point scale: good, fair, or poor. We recognize that this assessment is highly subjective; readers may take issue with particular values, or even the scale that we use. On the basis of the evidence, we grade life insurance as fair and annuities as poor. Life insurance earns a higher grade because it functions well for many people. But in both cases, there is some underinsurance, and in the case of life insurance some overinsurance as well.

EXPLANATIONS FOR POOR PERFORMANCE

Insurance in practice differs substantially from insurance in theory. Despite rating many insurance markets as likely to work well in theory, only one of the actual markets we evaluate draws a 'good' rating-homeowners insurance. Four markets get a fair rating (life insurance, short-term health insurance, auto insurance, and general business property and casualty insurance). The remaining six risks (annuities, long-term health risks, consumer durable insurance, and business environmental, terrorism and pension coverage) all rate poorly. While some may quibble with our ratings in particular cases, we suspect that none would disagree with our overall assessment of substantial underperformance in actual insurance markets.

The discrepancy between theory and practice is of two types. The first is a mismatch between expected coverage and actual coverage. Some risks that we expect to be covered, such as terrorism risk, long-term health risk, longevity risk, or environmental liability risk, are covered not at all, or at best poorly. Even risks that are covered well, such as life insurance, are not purchased by everyone who seems like they could benefit from them.

In contrast, many risks that theory would predict to be uncovered, such as small losses for automobiles, houses, and consumer durables, are covered by individuals voluntarily purchasing insurance. Assuming rational decision, only excessively high degrees of risk aversion could explain the pattern of property coverage that we observe. Further, many elderly seem overinsured against unexpected death (life insurance) even as they are underinsured against beyond-average survival (annuitization).

In addition, there is little rhyme or reason to the mix between public and private coverage. To be sure, many of the largest risks, such as terrorism, have made their way into the public sector, as one might expect. But smaller risks are covered publicly as well (flood insurance, for example), and many large risks are left to private insurers (environmental damage).

A common but troubling phenomenon is severe underpricing of risk coverage by the public sector, often because premiums are insufficiently responsive to risk differentials. Savings and loan insurance prior to the multi hundred billion dollar bailout is a good example. When politics and political pressures intrude, it is often impossible to impose significant differential rates for insurance. Often government just sets a risk standard to be met if one wants to insure. Such standards are often ambiguous, and government denial of insurance is often too much of a nuclear weapon.

The interactions between public and private insurance seem unhelpful at best, harmful at worst. There a number of complementary explanations for the mismatch between insurance theory and insurance markets in practice. We explore them in the next sections.

Information-Based Explanations

The explanation favored by most economists (casual polls suggest) is asymmetric information. Insurers may not offer particular products because they worry that it will affect the behavior of insureds (moral hazard), or because they fear that the product will be selected by people who have a high likelihood of suffering a loss (adverse selection). Such "bad behavior" cannot be monitored.

These explanations contribute, but we suspect that they are far from sufficient. For many of the risks that are uncovered, such as long-term environmental exposure by firms or the need for long-term care, evidence of moral hazard is at best tenuous. Where we are certain there is moral hazard is for use at a point in time, short-term health care for instance. This risk is covered, if anything, too well.

Nor is adverse selection much of an explanation. Evidence to date suggests no adverse selection in long-term care insurance purchases, for example (Finkelstein and McGarry, 2003). While adverse selection has dominated the theoretical literature, the actual experience of an insurer-what we think of as 'adverse experience'-depends on many factors beyond perceived risk. Risk aversion is important: the worried well purchase insurance just as much as the high risk. As a side benefit, this keeps premiums low for those on the margin of purchase.

Indeed, risk aversion may be inversely correlated with risk levels, if risk averse people take better care to avoid putting themselves in risky situations. Ignorance is also a blessing here. If potential insureds do not know their risk levels, there will be no correlation between risk and the insurance decision. More generally, non-rational behavior helps deter adverse selection. It introduces many new elements that encourage people to insure, without necessarily being correlated with risk. In many situations, we might expect that insurers would know more about risks than individuals. This is likely the case with consumer durable warranties, and possibly health insurance as well. Variation in price by risk status limit adverse selection, though they may be inefficient in other ways (denying people insurance over their risk level).

The limited explanatory power of asymmetric information-based explanations show up most clearly in the analysis of terrorism insurance. By all assessments, there is little to no differential information about the likelihood of terrorists striking any particular object (adverse selection) nor is it plausible that firms would substantially lower their guard against terrorist attack (moral hazard) just because they are insured. (The uncompensable losses, including one's own loss of life, are just too great.) Insurance coverage dried up for other reasons.

Our more general hypothesis is that in many markets where we might speculate that adverse selection would exert a powerful undertow on the market, it proves to be more mild current than sweeping tide. We propose three alternative reasons why the theory and practice of insurance diverge in the early 21st century.

Incomplete Diversification, Supply-side Contracting Difficulties

The first explanation is insufficient diversification of insurance companies. People may want insurance against a risk, but insurers have to be willing to provide that risk, even at rates far above the best estimates of actuarial cost. If insurers-or more accurately insurance executives--are worried about their capitalization, they may be unwilling to write policies for some risks, even if both price and demand are high. The prospect of severe losses, or even bankruptcy with its limited liability, may not scare the diversified investors in an insurance company, who would be happy to write unusual insurance for robust premiums. But insurance executives have to worry that they may be considered to have misestimated risks and premiums, with consequent career collapse. In the standard theory of insurance, risks are minimally correlated across insureds.

A few people will experience a loss in a period, but the vast majority will not. Insurers use the premiums from those who do not suffer a loss to compensate those who do. Many risks, however, have an aggregate component, many people incur a loss at the same time. Nuclear wars represented the ultimate aggregate risk for many years. Today's aggregate risks include new liability revolutions (as with environmental damage), significant increases in prices (say for medical care), and major terrorist attacks. Even good developments have their aggregate risk component. Thus, rapid rises in longevity would impose heavy aggregate costs on pensions and other annuities. Long-term care insurance well represents an aggregate risk: When the expected costs increase for one person, say because a longevity jump makes nursing home stays, particularly Alzheimer stays, more expensive, this factor applies to many insureds. As a result, the traditional method of risk diversification, pooling independent risks across people, fails.

Risk neutral insurers will not care about this aggregate risk. The owners of insurance company assets can diversify the risk posed by diversifying their portfolio. But managers and workers in those insurance companies may care. Their jobs may be lost if the company goes bankrupt, or if that line of business loses gobs of money. Thus, the insurance company itself may behave as if risk averse.

A moderately risk-averse insurance company will still sell insurance, but will impose a higher administrative charge to do so. Administrative loads in long-term care insurance, which has a large contingent of aggregate risk, are 35 percent at minimum, and reach 50 to 70 percent for some groups (Cutler, 1996; Brown and Finkelstein, 2003). In comparison, administrative costs in short-term health insurance are only about 15 percent (United States General Accounting Office, 1984), roughly their level for annuities (Mitchell, Poterba, Warshawsky, and Brown, 1999).

An insurer that is more risk averse than potential insureds will refuse to write insurance altogether. We often see this in the nature of risk exposure that is written. When they do write policies, long-term care insurers limit their exposure to a fixed dollar amount per day of nursing home care; one cannot buy coverage for the actual cost of care received (in contrast to annual health insurance). Similarly, environmental insurers and medical malpractice insurers refuse to cover all claims that result from operations today; instead, they put a time limit on when the claim must be filed.

The cycle of insurance crises shows clearly this problem. When risks increase more than expected-e.g., the liability revolution, knowledge of particular chemical harms, terrorist action-insurers respond at first by refusing to write new risk. That is understandable, as markets digest the new information. Over time, prices rise. That too is predictable. But even after the market 'settles down', insurance frequently becomes less generous than it was formerly, and stays that way indefinitely. That is the part that is economically unpredicted.

While the practice may appear to be irrational economically, the idea of severely curtailing company risk is standard advice given in the insurance industry. According to A.M. Best (1991), a leading analyst of the insurance industry, insurers should keep the risk of any line of business small. "[T]o provide stability and safety, an insurer should limit its maximum loss exposure on a single risk (or group of related risks) to a small percentage of its policyholders' surplus, normally less than 2 percent" (p. xiii). With aggregate risks, insurers face the Scylla and Charybdis of not knowing their market, or having too heavy exposure. The outcome is that the insurance industry does not write certain classes of risk.

For some risks the government may step in, as it has with terrorism risk. But that is a short-term (three-year) solution, it is as an adjunct to other private-sector insurance, and it is in an area where the government could be deemed to have responsibility for controlling the risk. Government as reinsurer is not a likely solution for many troubling aggregate risks, such as long-term environment or health-care risks.

Fortunately, there is a far greater pool of resources that could conceivably absorb such risks. It is found in financial markets. Risks that are large even for the world's insurance pool-estimated to be on the order of $1 trillion in the United States and $2 trillion worldwide (Insurance Information Institute, 2003)-are small relative to financial markets. For example, the value of equity markets in the US alone is more than $10 trillion. One great advantage of financial markets as insurance instruments, apart from their volume, is that they effectively bring together tens of millions of investors, none of whom would have to hold too much of an aggregate risk.

There has been recent use of financial markets to diversify aggregate insurance risks. Most prominent have been catastrophe bonds, used to reinsure weather-related housing risks. Interest in these bonds rose with Hurricane Andrew in 1992, the Northridge earthquake in 1994, and the Kobe, Japan earthquake in 1995, all involving losses that were massive relative to historical experience. The market for catastrophe bonds has been relatively small, but it is perceived to be successful (United States General Accounting Office, 2002). One measure of success is the prices charged. Famed investor Warren Buffett underwrote earthquake reinsurance in California for four years in the early 1990s, earning an 11 percent premium for an estimated 1 percent risk. Buffett recognized what other insurers must have missed: This risk, though unusual, brought neither adverse selection nor moral hazard. Over time, the advantage of this investment became known and premiums fell. "The influx of 'investor' money into catastrophe bonds-which may well live up to their name-has caused super-cat prices to deteriorate materially. Therefore, we will write less business in 1998", Buffett wrote.

Use of these new instruments is not without problems. Participation of insurance companies is likely to be important, since these companies have expertise in assessing risk that is vital. Possibly, insurance companies will underwrite the risks initially, to provide their assessment expertise for a fee, and investors will then take their share. Reinsurance is already common in the insurance industry, though it is typically done by specialized companies rather than broader financial markets.

Perhaps more importantly, the nature of the payment needs to be determined. Investment managers are currently paid for assuming risk. The common arrangement is for the general partner to charge an annual management fee, say 1 percent, and to receive 20 percent of the profits or excess profits.

With insurance, equivalent arrangements would be hard to structure, since risks are discrete and it is hard to know whether a policy issued has been profitable in expectation thus far. If there is a 3 percent chance of a calamitous event, for example, but otherwise no losses, a general partner paid on the basis of annual "profits" would be expected to do quite well for a period before the odds brought down the house. Further compounding the difficulty, prior management and incentive fees would probably be unrecoverable in the event of a bad loss. Many of the names at Lloyds of London experienced just such a string-many small successes followed by a mammoth loss-when the liability revolution hit.

One way around this problem would be to have the portfolio of risks be highly diversified. But such diversification blunts the value of specialized expertise on the market being insured. Other types of contracts may be needed. With additional time, we expect that financial instruments will continue to evolve and allow further investors into the market. It is possible-perhaps likely-that the first problem we identify has a solution forthcoming.

NON-STANDARD BEHAVIOR ON THE DEMAND SIDE

Theory and practice diverge in the insurance industry for a second reason: potential insureds engage in non-standard economic behavior. In traditional decision theory, people have concave utility functions defined over consumption. Risk averse people will want to insure against all risks, assuming fair actuarial pricing. They temper this because of moral hazard and administrative costs, which lead prices to exceed expected payouts. In response, people will choose to cover large risks, at least substantially, and leave small risks unprotected.

Such preferences may not correspond to reality, however, as the prevalence of insurance coverage for small risks suggests. Several alternatives to standard preferences have been proposed that may explain this type of coverage. Prospect theory. A leading possibility is loss aversion-the idea that people significantly dislike any loss, even small ones (Kahneman and Tversky, 1979). Hence, people will pay far above actuarial value to protect against small losses, such as those when a stereo breaks.

HEALTH

Health risk is the second major type of risk for individuals. We divide health risks into two categories: short-term risks, and long-term risks.

Short-term Health Risks

Most people have health insurance for current medical care needs. About 85 percent of people have some form of health insurance in the United States. Coverage rates are greater in most other major developed nations, usually because of government involvement.

As with mortality risk, there has been substantial analysis of the optimality of private health insurance contracts. The fact that not everyone has private insurance has generated policy debate and research attention. There are three typical explanations for lack of coverage. The first is administrative expense. In any market with administrative costs, we would expect coverage to be less than full. Administrative costs are only about 15 percent of health insurance, however, so most analysts discount this explanation. Indeed, the true rate of administrative expense in health insurance is likely smaller, perhaps net negative in many instances when buyer leverage is figured in. Health insurers-with their strong bargaining power in a high fixed-cost industry-purchase specific health care goods and services much more cheaply than do individuals. Such discounts likely more than make up for administrative costs.

Adverse selection provides a second explanation. Insurance priced for the average enrolled person can lead to an equilibrium where the healthy do not enroll. We know of no simulations about the importance of this phenomenon, but we suspect that this explanation is right for some people. Many of the uninsured are young and relatively healthy. The value of insurance priced at average rates would not be very high for this group. One concern about this explanation, though, is that insurance can vary along the intensive margin as well. Deductibles, services covered, and access to particular providers all vary across policies, and we might expect more of the healthy to segregate into less generous policies than go without coverage entirely. The third explanation is crowdout by government insurance programs (for example Medicaid) and charitable programs, e.g., hospital free care.

In this theory, people do not purchase private coverage because they know that they can receive care even if uninsured. Naturally, there is a loss. Being uninsured is associated with less, and less appealing, access to medical care providers, less use of preventive and acute care services, and worse health outcomes (Institute of Medicine, 2003). But it also saves money. For some people, the savings may be worth it. Empirical evidence shows that crowd-out is a factor in explaining insurance coverage. Increases in the generosity of public insurance (Cutler and Gruber, 1996), and in uncompensated care (Rask and Rask, 2000; Herring, 2001) lead more people to go uninsured. The type of analysis necessary to explain how much of the total number of uninsured this accounts for has not been undertaken, however.

Even were the level of health insurance appropriate, one might question the mix of provision between public and private. Insurance has a surprising mixture of such provision, in a pattern hardly in line with notions of comparative advantage across sectors. In the case of health insurance, some argue for public insurance, on the grounds that administrative costs are lower in public programs than in private policies (Woolhandler and Himmelstein, 1989).

Others argue for private insurance, for the usual reasons of competition and concern over bureaucracy. And within the private sector, there are arguments for both for-profit and not-for-profit entities. The US has a mixture of both public and private, often in the same narrow sector, with adverse interactions between the two (as witnessed by the crowd-out literature).

Among people who have insurance, economists' greatest concern has not been over inadequate coverage, but rather over the generosity of coverage people have for small medical risks. Cost sharing in traditional indemnity insurance policies is relatively low. A typical policy has a deductible of about $300, with 20 percent coinsurance up to a stop-loss of perhaps $1,500 (Kaiser Family Foundation and Health Research and Education Trust, 2003). For much of the health spending distribution, cost sharing will be very slight; this makes moral hazard a significant concern.

A lengthy literature has explored whether this structure of cost sharing is optimal or too small (see Cutler and Zeckhauser, 2000, for a review). Generally, the literature concludes that current insurance is too generous, leaving people with too little risk for medical expenses, particularly smaller expenses. The most comprehensive analysis is from Blomqvist (1997), who finds that optimal insurance should have a declining coinsurance rate ranging from 27 percent at $1,000 of spending (compared to 20 percent in most plans) down to 5 percent at $30,000 of spending (compared to zero in most plans). The traditional explanation for the low rate of cost sharing is the tax subsidy to health insurance (Feldstein and Friedman, 1977; Pauly, 1986). As with life insurance, employer payments for health insurance are not taxed as income to workers, while wage and salary payments are. Thus, there are incentives for people to run more medical payments through employer-paid health insurance than is optimal. This includes having lower cost-sharing than would otherwise be desirable. Empirical work shows that this explanation is important in practice (Cutler and Zeckhauser, 2000). What other factors contribute to low cost sharing is not known, however.

Behavioral explanations, which we explore at length subsequently, also merit study for low cost sharing. Fuchs (19xx), for example, argues that cost sharing is low in part because people do not want to make decisions about whether additional medical care is worth the money. We argue below that prospect-theoretic preferences for outcomes, e.g., loss aversion and risk seeking on losses, make individuals eager to avoid small losses.

We note that these types of behavioral explanations make normative analysis difficult. Say that loss aversion affected behavior, implying that even small per-visit charges strongly discourage use. Would such copayments represent an effective rationing tool, or would it be imposing noticeable pain without collecting much revenue? Fortunately, our analysis has a descriptive, not normative, purpose.

Finally, given HMOs strong penetration of the private insurance market and their firm supply-side restrictions, we note that it is hard to assess what appropriate cost sharing should be for their members.

Long-term Health-care Insurance

Health also has a long-term risk component. People may have health needs in the future, which they would like to insure today. Most important here is long-term care expenses; the magnitude of these expenses was noted earlier.

A large part of the return to long-term care insurance is related to early mortality among the elderly. Nearly 20 percent of people over age 85 are in a nursing home, compared to about 1 percent of the population aged 65 to 74. For long-term care insurance to be effective, people have to purchase before they reach advanced ages. Yet, most elderly do not have such coverage. Only about 10 percent of the elderly possess long-term care insurance. The bulk of long-term care expenses are paid for out-of-pocket or by Medicaid.

Risk about future health type is related to long-term care risk. Health insurance for individuals or the groups they buy as part of is usually experience rated. Should health decline, a person's (or their company's) premium increases. Thus, one might expect people to purchase insurance against the risk of becoming high cost in the future (Pauly, Kunreuther, and Hirth, 1995; Cochrane, 1995; Cutler, 1996). In practice, however, we see virtually no insurance against the risk of becoming sick and facing higher annual premiums in the future.

Adverse selection and moral hazard no doubt contribute to the failure of this market, but we believe the theoretical elegance of these subjects has led economists to give them too much weight. Risk aversion certainly differs across people, and that is not so correlated with health status (many of the worried well want to purchase insurance, in addition to the currently sick). Ex ante moral hazard is also somewhat deterred because health declines, even if treated, lead to much worse states, for which compensating payments are not forthcoming.

Attention has instead focused on two alternatives. The first is crowd-out of private long-term care insurance by the public sector. The Medicaid program covers long-term care expenses for people with no private insurance who have exhausted their income and assets paying for long-term care services. People may thus rely on Medicaid, if it comes to that, or give away assets to qualify for Medicaid, rather than purchase private insurance (Pauly, 1990). Recent simulation work suggests that this explanation can explain a significant fraction of the lack of purchase of private nursing home insurance (Brown and Finkelstein, 2003). As with short-term health insurance, there seems to be an inefficient interaction between public and private insurance.

The second explanation for low insurance coverage is that these risks are non-diversifiable, and thus shunned by insurance companies (Cutler, 1996). The dominant driver of changes in long-term care costs over time is technology that allows people to live longer or higher quality lives, but at high cost. This technology is common across people, and thus cannot be diversified cross-sectionally. We explore how this might affect the supply of long-term insurance below.

Summary. We rate coverage of short-term health risks as fair and coverage of long-term risks as poor. Short-term risks are covered for most people, but as with mortality risk there is both underprotection (those without coverage) and overprotection (too generous insurance in indemnity policies). Coverage for long-term health risks is poor, since private insurance is rare and the public sector has substantial inefficiencies.

Property

The third major type of individual risk is for property damage for personal physical assets. People insure their home, car, and consumer durables against various types of damages. In at least the first two cases, essentially everyone has coverage. Homeowners insurance is generally required by mortgage lenders, and all states require auto insurance. Fewer people have coverage for consumer durables, but the costs of these durables are far smaller, hence insurance is far less valuable.

The major issue in property insurance is the degree of cost sharing. Most people have relatively low deductibles for home and auto damage. The question is whether these deductibles are too low, from the standpoint of the individual and the standpoint of efficiency. (Efficiency requires avoiding little claims where administrative costs are large relative to any loss or payment.) There is speculation about this in the literature, but no formal analysis that we are aware of.

As with any evaluation dependent on the parameters of the utility function, we cannot say for certain whether consumers should or should not purchase more generous coverage. But we can evaluate what set of preferences are required to justify current purchases. Suppose that the probability of a loss is p. The loss may be damage to a car or house. For the simple algebra here, we assume the loss probability is independent of the details of the insurance policy.

INSURANCE IN PRACTICE-BUSINESS RISKS

Some markets for business risks seem to work well. Businesses own property, for example, and most businesses insure at least some portions of that property. There is not very good data on the extent of this insurance, but studies of the industry suggest that this insurance is generally believed to work well. This is not surprising, since large businesses have individuals who specialize in the purchase of insurance, and even small businesses usually have some financial expertise. Predominantly on a secondary reference basis, we rate this insurance as good on our scale.

Businesses also have general liabilities associated with damages they may incur in the cost of doing business (people falling in the store, for example, or doctors being sued over health harms they cause). The performance of this insurance varies by industry. If we take account of both drama and policy import, the situation is particularly problematic in medical malpractice.

There have been three medical malpractice crises in the past 25 years: one in the mid-1970s, another in the mid-1980s, and a third in just the past two years (Mello and Studdert, 2003). Each crisis was precipitated by claims paid increasing more rapidly than premium increases. The cause was changes in the social climate, not in any upswing in adverse medical incidents. Lawsuits filed increased more rapidly than expected, and liability judgments awarded were greater than expected.

As a result, insurers lost money. In response, premiums rose precipitously, many insurers dropped out of the market, many physicians found insurance difficult to obtain, and some physicians changed their practices (e.g., some OBGYNs quit doing obstetrics). Only after a few years did the market return to reasonable function, with insurance again available-albeit at higher price. This type of availability crisis, though often with no return to normalcy, is a common theme of many types of business insurance.

Risks with residual variability: environment and terrorism. In theory, as we noted above, insurance is best equipped to deal with small to moderate probability, high loss risks, for there is where it does the most good. However, it is for precisely those risks where business insurance has failed most recently. Environmental liability was the classic issue here (General Accounting Office, 1986; 1988; Huber, 1988; Zagaski, 1992); terrorism losses have recently joined it. In each case, private markets turned out to work much less well than anticipated, once the risks eventuated. We discuss these two risks in turn.

Prior to the mid-1980s, environmental coverage insured firms indefinitely for events that occurred during the policy year (termed an occurrence-based policy). Long-term risk was thought to be small. Total claims in the 1962, for example, were less than $XXX. Events in the 1970s and 1980s, however, highlighted the "long-tailed" nature of risk. Asbestos claims in the 1970s, for example, dealt with exposure to asbestos in the 1940s and 1950s. Added to this was the perception that legal interpretations were seen as changing the provisions of insurance policies. It was frequently asserted that courts ignored restrictions in policies to "sudden and accidental" environmental damage. Moreover, the courts, usually on the basis of jury decisions, imposed liabilities well beyond those the policy was intended to cover.

The result was increased uncertainty about the liability of environmental insurers.

In theory, an increase in risk should increase demand for insurance, increase the price of insurance, and result in greater overall coverage at higher prices. This was not the outcome with environmental risk, however, as it was not with medical malpractice insurance. Rather, the policies themselves changed in a way that made them less generous. For example, the occurrence-based policy was dropped in favor of a claims-made policy, which covers damages only if the claim is filed within a certain period of time.

Effectively, this eliminates insurance coverage for long-tail risk, placing that risk instead on the insuring firm, in the form of increases in premiums as the extent of damages is realized. Indeed, the reduction in insurance coverage was not limited to primary insurance markets. In 1984, international reinsurance markets began denying coverage for pollution liability reinsurance.

Insurers also imposed aggregate dollar limits on payouts for environmental damage, to limit their overall risk exposure. Of course, this is denying protection precisely where it is needed most, for high losses.

These changes limited the aggregate risk born by the insurer, with the consequence that more of the risk was retained by the firms at risk. Even two decades after the liability revolution and the initial cutbacks in insurance coverage, the market for environment insurance is substantially less generous than it was.

The 'crisis' in terrorism insurance burst onto the scene on September 11, 2001. The attacks that day drastically changed expectations about the likelihood and magnitude of terrorism losses in the future. Unlike nature's extreme blows, e.g., Hurricane Andrew, which can increase perceived future losses by say 100%, the man-made loss of 9/11 increased future expected terror losses at least by a factor of 10, perhaps much more. The immediate result was a crisis in insurance availability. Insurers claimed that terrorism was 'uninsurable', and stopped writing coverage for it. About one-quarter of policies written in 2002, an even larger share for large firms, excluded terrorist acts.

Though the most dire predictions about the consequences of lost insurance did not come true--buildings got built and buildings traded hands-the potential for severe economic disruption was judged to be high. After several months, the Federal government stepped in to stabilize the market. The Terrorism Risk Insurance Act of November 2002 provides for coverage related to international terrorism, with the Federal contribution rising with the magnitude of loss up through $100 billion of insured losses. Beyond that, the Congress decides what additional payments it wants to make.

In exchange for taking the back-end risk (without coinsurance), the Act requires insurers to write coverage for smaller terrorist losses. The Act sunsets at the end of 2005, and it is not clear what will happen in the market beyond that point. Employment practice insurance. Many businesses also have insurance for employment liability resulting from claims such as sexual harassment and race or gender lawsuits. As the potential liability from employment issues has become more widespread, the cost of this insurance has increased. As Table 6 shows, a business with 20 full-time employees and 20 part-time employees, for example, would pay a premium of $5,000 per year and have a 10 percent coinsurance rate.

There is also a limit on insurer liability, generally at $1,000,000. We do not know of general assessments of this line of insurance, however, so we omit it from the table. Pension obligations. One of the more important long-term risks that firms face is over their obligations to retirees. Many firms, particularly large manufacturers, have substantial defined benefit pension obligations. Firms also have obligations for retiree health insurance. These obligations are risky because retirement experience and the earnings on pension assets are both uncertain.

Insurance for these risks is affected by a substantial degree of moral hazard. Firms that are doing poorly have the option of declaring bankruptcy and defaulting on their pension liabilities, rather than continuing to pay them. As a result of this moral hazard, pension risk is insured by the government. The Pension Benefit Guarantee Corporation (PBGC) requires firms to contribute an annual premium based partly on the number of retirees and partly on the degree of pension underfunding.

Like many government programs, the PBGC has difficulty changing prices to guarantee solvency. This is particularly difficult since pension default is a long-tailed risk: premiums taken in today need to be saved for potentially high use in the future. Boyce and Ippolito (2002) estimate that premiums charged by the PBGC are 50 percent below what equivalent private insurance rates would be, with unfunded liabilities currently over $100 billion. For these reasons, the General Accounting office rated the PBGC as high-risk.

Because participation in the PBGC is mandatory, we lose the yardstick of what private insurance would charge for equivalent coverage. And because it is effectively subsidized, there is little complaint. For these reasons, we rate the operation of pension insurance as poor.

Summary. Businesses are much more sophisticated than individuals about the purchase of insurance, with professionals handling the task in large firms. For traditional risks, insurance works well. Recent years, however, have witnessed the rise of risks due to purposeful human activity, e.g., the liability revolution or terrorism. These risks are larger than older risks, are correlated across insuring firms, and are often not resolved for many years. For such risks, insurance markets tend to work poorly.

CONCLUSION

In November 2003, the Medicare program, set up in the 1960s and largely the same today as then, was enriched by the addition of an outpatient prescription drug benefit. In many ways, adding prescription drugs to Medicare represented a triumph of economic reasoning. The fundamental principle of insurance demand is that coverage becomes more valuable as the variability of potential outcomes grows. In the 1960s, prescription drug costs were low, and there was little risk associated with buying medications. It made little sense to include prescription drugs in coverage. By 2003, the risks for the elderly were much greater. Even though the costs to the government of the new benefit were high, the potential risk-spreading value made it worthwhile. We also identify possible solutions. Encouraging greater risk spreading beyond the narrow confines of primary insurance and reinsurance is a central one.

Sometimes, government and private firms collaborate in this venture, as in terrorism insurance, where the government is a reinsurer. More generally, financial markets represent an enormous pool of largely-untapped potential insurance dollars. The future, we are confident, will confront significant new risks, and will develop new mechanisms for spreading them. Alas, neither the invisible hand nor sophisticated theories of insurance will assure that the right entities write the right coverage for the right insureds. Our theories of insurance must be elaborated to capture realities on the ground, including the factors that motivate entities to insure. Insurance practice should be adjusted to meet realistic expectations of how risks can be spread effectively.

This ongoing minuet of adjustments, perhaps a dance over decades, should allow the theory and practice of insurance to reunite. Alas, effective risk sharing was not fully enshrined in the new legislation. Indeed, the cost sharing in the new legislation is, by economic considerations, somewhat bizarre. Elderly enrolling in the new program face a $250 deductible. After that, the government pays 25 percent of the bill up to $2,250 in total spending. The government then ceases payment until total spending reaches $5,100 ($3,600 of individual costs). Above that amount, the government pays 95 percent and the individual 5 percent. There is no upper limit on individual spending. From a risk-spreading perspective, a far more valuable insurance policy would have individuals cover more of the up-front costs, and leave the government to take more of the back-end liability. Politics no doubt helps to explain the benefits structure, probably derived from the type of utility anomalies discussed above. A certainty equivalent benefit of $110, where the actual monies go to 10 percent of the elderly population may be politically less effective than a certainty equivalent benefit of $100 where a large share of the money is spent among the vast part of the population.

The new legislation also considers the issue of public and private insurance, but here too the answer seems strange. Why didn't the private sector ever offer insurance for prescription drugs if that coverage is so valuable? The answer is that drug benefits are almost a poster child for adverse selection. The elderly with high drug needs know who they are, and they would raise the cost of private drug coverage beyond what the vast majority of elderly would consider paying. Given sufficient skewness in expenditure, the market unravels. Still, the new legislation envisions the majority of the elderly obtaining coverage through private insurance companies offering stand-alone pharmaceutical coverage. The classic economic solution to adverse selection-single payer health insurance-was explicitly rejected as being too regulatory a solution. To partly offset the selection incentives induced, the legislation includes a substantial sum to give to employers already providing drug coverage-28 percent of costs between $250 and $5,000 per person. It is not known if this subsidy will prevent crowdout any more than previous subsidies to the poor through Medicaid.

Unfortunately (for economists), the seeming anomalies in the Medicare drug benefit are more common than we would care to admit. Exploring a number of insurance policies in practice, we argue that the conventional theory of insurance misses reality in two respects. First, it assumes near risk neutrality on the supply-side of the market, when in fact strong risk aversion is more appropriate, particularly given agency concerns of insurance decision makers. Second, we show that many attributes of insurance equilibrium can best be explained if people's behavior diverges from the rational model. They have non-standard preferences-e.g., they care about even tiny losses; they seek to equate utility across states not marginal utility; they disproportionately buy coverage for risks that are "available".

2

PRINCIPLES OF THE LIFE INSURANCE

INTRODUCTION

Insurable Interest The insured must have insurable interest in the life assured. In absence of insurable interest, Contract of insurance is void. Insurable interest must be present at the time of entering into contract with insurance company for life insurance. It is not necessary that the assured should have insurable interest at the time of maturity also.

Insurable interest exists in the following cases:

(a) A person has an unlimited insurable interest in his/her own life.

(b) A person has an insurable interest in the life of his/her spouse.

(c) A father has an insurable interest in the life of his son or daughter on whom he is dependent. Likewise a son may have insurable interest in life of his parents.

(d) A creditor has an insurable interest in the life of the debtor, to the extent of the debt.

(e) A servant employed for a specified period has insurable interest in the life of his employer.

Utmost Good Faith

The contract of life insurance is a contract of utmost good faith. The insured should be open and truthful and should not conceal any material fact in giving information to the insurance company, while entering into a contract with insurance company. Misrepresentation or concealment of any fact will entitle the insurer to repudiate the contract if he wishes to do so.

Not a Contract of Indemnity

The life insurance contract is not a contract of indemnity. A Contract of life insurance is not a contract of indemnity. The loss of life cannot be compensated and only a fixed sum of money is paid in the event of death of the insured. So, the life insurance contract is not a contract of indemnity. The loss resulting from the death of life assured cannot be calculated in terms of money.

IMPORTANCE OF LIFE INSURANCE.

Life Insurance is of great importance to individuals, groups, business community and general public. Some of the main benefits of life insurance are given below.

Protection against untimely Death

Life insurance provides protection to the dependents of the life insured and the family of the assured in case of his untimely death. The dependents or family members get a fixed sum of money in case of death of the assured.

Saving for Old Age

After retirement the earning capacity of a person reduces. Life insurance enables a person to enjoy peace of mind and a sense of security in his/her old age.

Promotion of Savings

Life insurance encourages people to save money compulsorily. When a life policy is taken, the assured is to pay premiums regularly to keep the policy in force and he cannot get back the premiums, only surrender value can be returned to him. In case of surrender of policy, the policyholder gets the surrendered value only after the expiry of duration of the policy.

Initiates Investments

Life Insurance Corporation encourages and mobilizes the public savings and channelises the same in various investments for the economic development of the country. Life insurance is an important tool for the mobilization and investment of small savings.

Credit Worthiness

Life insurance policy can be used as a security to raise loans. It improves the credit worthiness of business.

Social Security

Life insurance is important for the society as a whole also. Life insurance enables a person to provide for education and marriage of children and for construction of house. It helps a person to make financial base for future.

Tax Benefit

Under the Income Tax Act, premium paid is allowed as a deduction from the total income under section 80C.

Types of Life Insurance Policies

Life insurance policies can be grouped into the following categories:

TERM POLICY

In case of Term assurance plans, insurance company promises the insured for a nominal premium to pay the face value mentioned in the policy in case he is no longer alive during the term of the policy. Term assurance policy has the following features:

- It provides a risk cover only for a prescribed period. Usually these policies are short-term plans and the term ranges from one year onwards. If the policyholder survives till the end of this period, the risk cover lapses and no insurance benefit payment is made to him.

- The amount of premium to be paid for these policies is lower than all other life insurance policies.

  As savings and reserves are not accumulated under this policy, it has no surrender value and loan or paid-up values are not allowed on these policies.
- This plan is most suitable for those who are initially unable to pay high premium
- when income is low as required for Whole Life or Endowment policies, but requires life cover for a high amount.

WHOLE LIFE POLICY

This policy runs for the whole life of the assured. The sum assured becomes payable to the legal heir only after the death of the assured. The whole life policy can be of three types.

(1) Ordinary whole life policy – In this case premium is payable periodically throughout the life of the assured.

(2) Limited payment whole life policy – In this case premium is payable for a specified period (Say 20 Years or 25 Years) Only.

(3) Single Premium whole life policy – In this type of policy the entire premium is payable in one single payment.

ENDOWMENT LIFE POLICY

In this policy the insurer agrees to pay the assured or his nominees a specified sum of money on his death or on the maturity of the policy which ever is earlier.

The premium for endowment policy is comparatively higher than that of the whole life policy. The premium is payable till the maturity of the policy or until the death of the assured which ever is earlier. It provides protection to the family against the untimely death of the assured.

HEALTH INSURANCE SCHEMES

An individual is subject to uncertainty regarding his health. He may suffer from ailments, diseases, disability caused by stroke or accident, etc. For serious cases the person may have to be hospitalized and intensive medical care has to be provided which can be very expensive. It is here that medical insurance is helpful in reducing the financial burden.

These days the vulnerability to lifestyle diseases such as heart, cancer, neurotic, and pollution based, etc are on the increase. So it makes sense for an individual to go for medical insurance cover.

JOINT LIFE POLICY

This policy is taken on the lives of two or more persons simultaneously. Under this policy the sum assured becomes payable on the death of any one of those who have taken the joint life policy. The sum assured will be paid to the survivor(s). For example, a joint life policy may be taken on the lives of husband and wife, sum assured will be payable to the survivor on the death of the spouse.

WITH PROFIT AND WITHOUT PROFIT POLICY

Under with profit policy the assured is paid, in addition to the sum assured, a share in the profits of the insurer in the form of bonus.

Without profit policy is a policy under which the assured does not get any share in the profits earned by the insurer and gets only the sum assured on the maturity of the policy. With profit and without profit policies are also known as participating and non –participating policies respectively.

DOUBLE ACCIDENT BENEFIT POLICY

This policy provides that if the insured person dies of any accident, his beneficiaries will get double the amount of the sum assured.

ANNUITY POLICY

Under this policy, the sum assured is payable not in one lump sum payment but in monthly, quarterly and half-yearly or yearly installments after the assured attains a certain age. This policy is useful to those who want to have a regular income after the expiry of a certain period e.g. after retirement. Annuity is paid so long as the assured survives. In annuity policy medical checkup is not required. Annuity is paid so long as the assured survives.

POLICIES FOR WOMEN

Women, now a days are free to take life assurance policies. However, some specially designed policies suit their needs in a unique manner; the synopsis of some these policies are as follows:

a. Jeevan Sathi is also known a Life Partner plan where the husband and wife are covered under this endowment policy, which gives the following benefits.

    i. On maturity, provided both are alive, full sum assured with bonus is paid.

    ii. On the death of one of the assured during the period of the policy, basic sum assured is paid to the surviving partner, who is not required to pay any further premiums.

    iii. The surviving partner remains covered for the full sum assured. If she/he dies, then the sum assured is paid to the nominee, but this is before the maturity date.

    iv. The surviving partner will be paid sum assured with bonuses if he survives till the maturity date. Hence this policy gives a comprehensive family protection.

b. Jeevan Sukanya is highlighted by the following points.

    i. Only female child aged between 1 to 12 years is covered in this plan.

ii. band is automatically covered under the policy after marriage.

iii. Risk of the child starts either after 2 years of taking the policy or not before the age of 7, whichever is early.

iv. Premium paying period is 20 years minus age at entry.

v. On surviving the age of 20, the life assured receives the sum assured as survival benefit and the policy continues to cover the life assured till maturity date when vested bonus will be paid only. If life assured dies before maturity, sum assured with bonuses will be paid.

GROUP INSURANCE

Group life insurance is a plan of insurance under which the lives of many persons are covered under one life insurance policy. However, the insurance on each life is independent of that on the other lives. Usually, in group insurance, the employer secures a group policy for the benefit of his employees. Insurer provides coverage for many people under single contract.

POLICIES FOR CHILDREN

Policies for children are meant for the various needs of the children such as education, marriage, security of life etc. Some of the major children policies are:

(1) Children's deferred assurances

(2) Marriage endowment and educational annuity plans

(3) Children endowment policy

MONEY BACK POLICY

In this case policy money is paid to the insured in a number of separate cash payments. Insurer gives periodic payments of survival benefit at fixed intervals during the term of policy as long as the policyholder is alive.

Documentation

The contract for the life insurance starts with the proposal made by the proposer in standard application form available with insurance company and then various other documents are prepared.

PROPOSAL FORMS

The proposal form is a standardized form. The proposal form is a type of an application form, which a proposer has to fill all the relevant details about the life to be assured. The agent has the proposal form with him provided by the insurer. There are different types of policies and so the different types of proposal forms are there. It has the entire details regarding the duration of the policy, type of plan, mode of payment, etc. A proposal form is to be to be completed by the proposer in his own handwriting and signed in the presence of the agent. The proposal form contains a declaration at the end, to ensure the authenticity of the information given.

Usually the proposal form contains the following information to be filled by the prospective insured:

1. Name of life assured
2. Address
3. Date of Birth
4. Occupation
5. Age
6. Name of the employer (if any)
7. Sum assured of the proposed policy
8. Number and age of the family members
9. Family medical history
10. Proposer's Medical history

Besides these there are other related forms regarding health, occupation, the agent's confidential report and many others. In addition there is a consent letter which shows the consent of the life assured to the imposition of some clause or extra premium, duly signed by the life assured.

FIRST PREMIUM RECEIPT

The agent provides the proposal form and other related documents and the underwriter examines the form and other documents and then determines the terms on which to accept the risk or reject the same.

The consent of the person assured is obtained in the form of payment of premium. After receiving the payment, the insurance company issues the First Premium Receipt, which acknowledges the proposal of the life-assured. It contains all particulars of the policy. It has the details of the next premium to be paid.

The policy bond is sent within 45-50 days from the date of first premium receipt to the life assured. The First Premium Receipt is an important and powerful document on the basis of which the life-assured can ask the insurer to issue the policy bond, which is treated as Evidence of the Contract of Life assurance.

POLICY BOND

After issuing the First Premium Receipt, the next step is that of the insurer of sending the policy bond to the life-assured and this document is also known as Policy Contract, which is the ultimate evidence of the life-assured.

The Policy Contract contains all the terms and conditions of the contract between insurance company and the life assured, duly stamped as per the Indian Stamp Act. The policy is sent to the life assured by the insurer. The policy contract contains the details of the insurance such as duration of the policy, the type of policy, sum assured, premium amount and the date of maturity, extra premium, nominee, assignee etc.

ALTERATIONS AND ENDORSEMENTS

Endorsement is an authenticated noting on the back of Policy Contract and forms a part of the contract. In the case of lack of space, the endorsements can be put on a separated sheet of papers and attached to the policy. Endorsements are required because life assurance is a long-term contract and the life assured may want certain changes in the terms of contract.

There are different type of alterations or modifications that can be made during the tenure of the policy such as changes regarding increase or reduction in the sum assured, mode of payment of premium, modification related on account of mistakes in the preparation of the policy by the insurer, modifications related to reduction in term, conversion from "Non-profit" to "With Profit" and similar other like change of name, plan-term and so on.

REMINDING NOTICE

It is basically information sent by the insurer to the policyholder, reminding the latter about the due date of a particular premium and the amount of premium. However it is not the duty of the insurance company (insurer) to do so. The insurer also informs the policyholder about the lapse of a policy if the premiums are not paid in time.

OTHER DOCUMENTS

Apart from other documents there are some other specialized documents, which are as follows:

i. Proposal on the lives of Non Resident Indians, which consists of some special questionnaire asking for relevant information.

ii. Partnership Insurance which consist of papers asking for the Profit & Loss account of the firm for the last three years, the insurance of the partner, the partnership deed and the deed of variation allowing the purchase of the assurance policy.

Settlement of Claims

The easy and timely settlement of a valid claim is an important function of an insurance company. The yardstick to judge insurance company's efficiency is as to how quick the claim settlement is. The speed, kindness and fairness with which an insurer handles claims show the maturity of the company and may lead to great satisfaction of the client. In every insurance company claim handling is of immense importance. It is the liability of the insurance company to honour valid and legal claims. At the same the company must identify the fraudulent and invalid claims. A claim may arise:

i) On death of Policyholder before the maturity date.

ii) On maturity, i.e. after expiry of the endowment period specified in the policy contract when the policy money becomes payable.

Certain features are common to all life insurance claims. These are:

1. Policy must be in force at the time of claims.
2. Insured must be covered by the policy.
3. Nothing was outstanding to the insurer at the time of claim.
4. Claim is covered by the policy.

DEATH CLAIMS

Intimation of Death

The death of the life assured has to be intimated in writing to the insurer. It can be done by the Assignee or nominee under the policy or from a person representing such Assignee or Nominee or when there is no nomination or assignment by a relative of the life assured, the employer, the agent or the development officer. Where policy is assigned to a creditor or a bank for valuable consideration, intimation of death may be received from such assignee. Sometimes, the office need not wait till the intimation of claim is received. The concerned agent, newspaper reports in case of accidents or air crashes, obituary columns may give information and claim action can be started. However, the identity of the deceased should be established carefully. The intimation of the death of the life assured by the claimant should contain the following particulars:

(1) his or her relationship with the deceased,

(2) the name of the policyholder,

(3) the number/s of the policy/policies,

(4) the date of death

(5) the cause of death and

(6) sum assured etc.

If any of these particulars are missing the claimant can be asked to furnish the same to the insurer. The intimation must satisfy two conditions (1) It must establish properly the identity of the deceased person as the life assured under the policy, (2) It must be from a concerned person.

Proof of Death and Other Documents

In case of claim by death, after the receiving the intimation of death the insurance company ensures that the insurance policy has been in force for the sum assured on the date of death and the intimation has been received from assignee, nominee or other claimant.

The following documents are required:

(i) Certificate of death.

(ii) Proof of age of the life assured (if not already given).

(iii) Deeds of assignment / reassignments.

(iv) Policy document.

(v) Form of discharge.

If the claim has accrued within three years from the beginning of the policy, the following additional requirements may be called for:

(i) Statement from the hospital if the deceased had been admitted to hospital.

(ii) Certificate of medical attendant of the deceased giving details of his/her last illness.

(iii) Certificate of cremation or burial to be given by a person of known character and responsibility present at the cremation or burial of the body of the deceased.

(iv) Certificate by employer if the deceased was an employee.

Proof of death and other documents to be submitted will depend upon the cause of death and circumstances of each case.

(1) In case of an air crash the certificate from the airline authorities would be necessary certifying that the assured was a passenger on the plane. In case of ship accident a certified extract from the logbook of the ship is required. In case of sudden cardiac arrest, murder the doctors' certificate may not be available.

(2) The insurance may waive strict evidence of title if the sum assured of the policy is small and there is no dispute among the survivors of the policy moneys.

(3) If the life assured had a death due to accident, suicide or unknown cause the police inquest report, panchanama. post mortem report, etc would be required.

If by any chance policy contract is lost, advertisement of the lost of policy is to be given. Payment can be made on the basis of an indemnity given by the policyholder. If the deceased has taken out policies with more than one branch and the claimant has produced proof of death to any one of them and desires that the other branch or branches, may act on the same proof, his request should be complied with. The Branch requiring proof of death should directly call for the certified copies from the branch concerned.

Net Payable Amount of Claim

After receiving the required documents the company calculates the amount payable under the policy. For this purpose, a form is filled in which the particulars of the policy, assignment, nomination, bonus etc. should be entered by reference to the Policy Ledger Sheet.

If a loan exists under the policy, then the section dealing with loan is contacted to give the details of outstanding loan and interest amount, which is deducted from the gross policy amount to calculate net payable claim amount.

The net amount of claim payable is calculated and is called payment voucher. In the case of 'in force' policy unpaid premiums if any due before the Assured's death with late fee where necessary and the premium falling due in the policy year current at the time of death should be deducted from the claim amount.

MATURITY CLAIMS

If the life insured survives to the full term, then basic sum assured is payable. This payment by the insurer to the insured on the date of maturity is called maturity payment. The amount payable at the time of the maturity includes a sum assured and bonus/incentives.

The insurer sends in advance the intimation to the insured with a blank discharge form for filling various details in it. It is to be returned to the office along with

- Original Policy document
- Age proof if age is not already submitted
- Assignment /reassignment, if any..

Legally no claim is acceptable in respect for a lapsed policy or death of the Life assured happening within 3 years from the date of beginning of the policy. However, some concessions are given and payment of claims is made:

- If the Life assured had paid at least 3 years' premiums and thereafter if premiums have not been paid, the nominees/life assured get proportionate paid up value.
- In the event of the death of' the Life assured within 3 years and the policy is under the lapsed position, nothing is payable.

PROCEDURE OF THE MATURITY CLAIMS

Settlement procedure for maturity claim is simple after receipt of completed and stamped discharge form from the person entitled to the policy money along with policy documents, claim amount will be paid by account payee cheque.

- If the life assured is reported to have died after the date of maturity but before the receipt is discharged, the claim is to be treated as the maturity claim and paid to the legal heirs. In this case death certificate and evidence of title is required.
- Where the assured is known to be mentally deranged, a certificate from the court of law under the Indian Lunacy Act appointing a person to act as guardian to manage the properties of the lunatic should be called.

ADDITIONAL BENEFITS APART FROM REGULAR CLAIMS

Double Accident Benefit: For claiming the benefits under the Double Accident Benefit the claimant has to produce the proof to the satisfaction of the Corporation that the accident is defined as per the policy conditions. Normally for claiming this benefit documents like FIR, Post-mortem Report are required.

Disability Benefit Claims include waiver of all premiums to be paid in future till the expiry of the policy of the life assured if a person is totally and permanently disabled and cannot earn any wage/compensation/profit as a result of the accident. Presently, all over the country there are 12 centers where the Insurance Ombudsman has been appointed. They are part of grievance redressal machinery. They consider the complaints regarding disputes related to premiums, claims etc.

UNDER WRITING AND SERVICING

Underwriting of New Business

One of the most important functions of the New Business Department is to decide whether to accept, postpone or decline a risk and to determine the terms to be offered if the risk is to be accepted. This is called underwriting or selection of risk. The underwriter has to evaluate the hazards associated with the risk, which is being proposed.

The life insurance underwriting is concerned with mortality rate and risk, i.e., the risk that the life insured may die before the maturity of the policy. Mortality risk depends upon the life insured's health, family medical history, nature of work etc. Underwriting is the insurance function that is responsible for assessing and classifying the degree of risk a proposer has and then deciding whether to accept or reject the risk.

UNDERWRITING PROCESS

The person willing to purchase the life insurance policy fills the proposal form. The proposal form along with the medical examiner's report and the other reports is checked and the risk associated with the case is calculated. After evaluation of risk, the insurer has following choices:

The insurance company may accept the proposal.

If a company decides to accept then the calculation regarding the premium to be charged from the proposer is to be made and terms and conditions are decided upon. The premium should be paid within a particular period specified by the insurer failing which the proposal stands cancelled.

The insurance company may reject the proposal

If the company decides not to accept the proposal then the proposer is informed accordingly. If the insurer decides to accept the proposal on special terms the proposer is informed accordingly.

The process of underwriting consists of following steps:

EVALUATION OF DOCUMENTS

1. The proposal papers will be complete when the proposal forms; medical examiner's report, agent's confidential report and personal statement are attached. In some cases medical examination may not be required. The

question sin the proposal form must be answered with full honesty and no material fact should be concealed. The following particulars are generally required by the insurer:

i) Age, Sex, Height and weight.

ii) Occupation: The detailed information can be asked about the occupation if considered hazardous like aviation, electrical and chemical industry.

iii) Other Policies: The number and amount of other policies of the proposer.

iv) Premium to be paid and income of the proposer should be consistent, i.e., ensuring that proposer will not have any problem paying the premium of the policy.

v) Date of Birth: The proposer who is either less than 20 years of age or more than 50 years of age should give satisfactory proof of age.

vi) Risky habits of the proposer (Car racing etc)

vii) Alcohol intake (Excessive intake of alcohol may affect the death probability of the proposer)

viii) Frequency of foreign travel

ix) Marital status and number of children of proposer

x) Medical examiner's report

LIFE INSURANCE, INDIA

Life is very fragile and death is a certainty. We cannot control the uncertainties of life. But, we can cover the risks surrounding us. Life insurance, simply put, is the cover for the risks that we run during our lives. It protects us from the contingencies that could affect us.

Life insurance is not for the person who passes away, it for those who survive. It is the responsibility of every bread earner to guard against the events that could affect the family in the unfortunate circumstance of his / her demise. Thus, having a life insurance policy is very vital. Before going for a life insurance policy it is imperative that you know about various types of life insurance policies. Major among them are:

- Endowment Policy
- Whole Life Policy
- Term Life Policy
- Money-back Policy
- Joint Life Policy
- Group Insurance Policy
- Loan Cover Term Assurance Policy
- Pension Plan or Annuities
- Unit Linked Insurance Plan

Endowment Policy, India

An endowment policy covers risk for a specified period, at the end of which the sum assured is paid back to the policyholder, along with the bonus accumulated during the term of the policy. An endowment life insurance policy is designed primarily to provide a living benefit and only secondarily to provide life insurance protection. Therefore, it is more of an investment than a whole life policy.

Endowment life insurance pays the face value of the policy either at the insured's death or at a certain age or after a number of years of premium payment. Endowment policy is an instrument of accumulating capital for a specific purpose and protecting this savings program against the saver's premature death.

Whole Life Insurance Policy, India

A whole life policy runs as long as the policyholder is alive. As risk is covered for the entire life of the policyholder, therefore, such policies are known as whole life policies. A simple whole life policy requires the insurer to pay regular premiums throughout the life. In a whole life policy, the insured amount and the bonus is payable only to the nominee of the beneficiary upon the death of the policyholder. There is no survival benefit as the policyholder is not entitled to any money during his / her own lifetime.

Term Life Insurance Policy, India

Term life insurance policy covers risk only during the selected term period.

If the policyholder survives the term, the risk cover comes to an end. Term life policies are primarily designed to meet the needs of those people who are initially unable to pay the larger premium required for a whole life or an endowment assurance policy.

No surrender, loan or paid-up values are granted under term life policies because reserves are not accumulated. If the premium is not paid within the grace period, the policy lapses without acquiring any paid-up value.

Money Back Policy, India

Money back policy provides for periodic payments of partial survival benefits during the term of the policy, as long as the policyholder is alive.

They differ from endowment policy in the sense that in endowment policy survival benefits are payable only at the end of the endowment period.

An important feature of money back policies is that in the event of death at any time within the policy term, the death claim comprises full sum assured without deducting any of the survival benefit amounts, which may have already been paid as money-back components. The bonus is also calculated on the full sum assured.

Joint Life Insurance Policy, India

Joint life insurance policies are similar to endowment policies as they too offer maturity benefits to the policyholders, apart form covering risks like all life insurance policies.

But joint life policies are categorized separately as they cover two lives simultaneously, thus offering a unique advantage in some cases, notably, for a married couple or for partners in a business firm.

Under a joint life policy the sum assured is payable on the first death and again on the death of the survivor during the term of the policy. Vested bonuses would also be paid besides the sum assured after the death of the survivor. If one or both the lives survive to the maturity date, the sum assured as well as the vested bonuses are payable on the maturity date. The premiums payable cease on the first death or on the expiry of the selected term, whichever is earlier.

Group Insurance, India

Group insurance offers life insurance protection under group policies to various groups such as employers-employees, professionals, co-operatives, weaker sections of society, etc. It also provides insurance coverage for people in certain approved occupations at the lowest possible premium cost.

Group insurance plans have low premiums. Such plans are particularly beneficial to those for whom other regular policies are a costlier proposition. Group insurance plans extend cover to large segments of the population including those who cannot afford individual insurance.

A number of group insurance schemes have been designed for various groups. These include employer-employee groups, associations of professionals (such as doctors, lawyers, chartered accountants etc.), members of cooperative banks, welfare funds, credit societies and weaker sections of society.

Loan Cover Term Assurance Policy, India

Loan cover term assurance policy is an insurance policy, which covers a home loan. Such a policy covers the individual's home loan amount in case of an eventuality. The cover on such a policy keeps reducing with the passage of time as individuals keep paying their EMIs (equated monthly instalments) regularly, which reduces the loan amount.

This plan provides a lumpsum in case of death of the life assured during the term of the plan. The lumpsum will be a decreasing percentage of the initial sum assured as per the policy schedule. Since this is a non-participating (without profits) pure risk cover plan, no benefits are payable on survival to the end of the term of the policy.

Various insurance companies offering loan repayment protection insurance policy are

- HDFC Standard Life Insurance
- Tata AIG
- ING Vysya
- LIC

Pension Plan, India

A pension plan or an annuity is an investment that is made either in a single lump sum payment or through installments paid over a certain number of years, in return for a specific sum that is received every year, every half-year or every month, either for life or for a fixed number of years.

Annuities differ from all the other forms of life insurance in that an annuity does not provide any life insurance cover but, instead, offers a guaranteed income either for life or a certain period.

Typically annuities are bought to generate income during one's retired life, which is why they are also called pension plans. By buying an annuity or a pension plan the annuitant receives guaranteed income throughout his life. He also receives lump sum benefits for the annuitant's estate in addition to the payments during the annuitant's lifetime.

Unit Linked Insurance Plans (ULIP)

Unit linked insurance plan (ULIP) is life insurance solution that provides for the benefits of protection and flexibility in investment. The investment is denoted as units and is represented by the value that it has attained called as Net

Asset Value (NAV). The policy value at any time varies according to the value of the underlying assets at the time.

ULIP provides multiple benefits to the consumer. The benefits include:

- Life protection
- Investment and Savings
- Flexibility
- Adjustable Life Cover
- Investment Options
- Transparency
- Options to take additional cover against
- Death due to accident
- Disability
- Critical Illness
- Surgeries
- Liquidity
- Tax planning

Insurance Companies in India

Before insurance sector was opened to the private sector Life Insurance Corporation (LIC) was the only insurance company in India. After the opening up of Insurance sector in India there has been a glut of insurance companies in India. These companies have come up with innovative and flexible insutrance policies to cater to varying needs of the individual. Opening up of the Insurance sector has also forced the Lic to tighten up its belt and deliver better service. All in all it has been a bonanza for the consumer.

Major Life insurance Companies in India are:

- Aviva Life Insurance
- Bajaj Allianz
- Birla S un Life Insurance

- HDFC Standard Life Insurance
- ICICI Prudential
- ING Vysya
- Kotak Mahindra
- LIC
- Max New York Life Insurance
- Metlife India Insurance
- Reliance Life Insurance
- SBI Life Insurance
- Shriram Life Insurance
- Tata AIG Life Insurance

General Insurance, India

General Insurance provides much-needed protection against unforeseen events such as accidents, illness, fire, burglary et al. Unlike Life Insurance, General Insurance is not meant to offer returns but is a protection against contingencies. Almost everything that has a financial value in life and has a probability of getting lost, stolen or damaged, can be covered through General Insurance policy.

Property (both movable and immovable), vehicle, cash, household goods, health, dishonesty and also one's liability towards others can be covered under general insurance policy. Under certain Acts of Parliament, some types of insurance like Motor Insurance and Public Liability Insurance have been made compulsory.

Major insurance policies that are covered under General Insurance are:

1-Home Insurance

2-Health Insurance

3-Motor Insurance

4-Travel Insurance

Home Insurance, India

Every man has a dream to own a house one day. For an ordinary person it takes a whole lifetime of savings to build a house. And one cannot predict a natural calamity like earthquake. In recent times we have seen what havoc an earthquake or any other natural calamity such as floods, landslides and torrential rains can wreck. Hence home insurance is very important. Home insurance policy also protects against other hazards like gas cylinder explosion, fire due to electric short circuit as well as man-made disaster like burglary.

Home insurance policy available in the market covers broadly two things:

- Building structure
- Contents inside the home

Insurance Covers for a Building Structure are:

The Fire and Special Perils Cover

This is a comprehensive packaged cover that covers damages to the structure of home due to

- Fire
- Storm, tempest, flood & inundation
- Riot, strike & malicious damage
- Lightning
- Explosion & implosion
- Aircraft damage
- Damage due to impact by vehicles
- Subsidence, landslides and rockslides
- Bursting and/or overflowing of water tanks, apparatus and pipes
- Missile testing operation
- Leakage from automatic Sprinkler installations
- Bush fire

Earthquake Cover

Covers damages to the structure of your house due to earthquake

Terrorism Cover

Covers damages to the structure of your house due to acts of terrorism. A home insurance does not cover the market value of the home. The price of the home includes the cost of the land and the cost of constructing the building structure on this land and the land cannot be insured. The insurance cover is only for the cost of constructing the building. The sum insured is calculated by multiplying your home area by the construction rate per sq. feet.

Insurance Cover for Contents Inside the Home

This cover is only for damages or loss of the contents inside the home-electronic and electrical goods, furniture and fixtures, clothing, jewelry and any other contents inside the home.

The covers that can be taken for the contents are as follows:

- The Fire and Specials Perils Cover
- Earthquake Cover
- Burglary
- Loss / damage to contents due to burglary or an attempted burglary
- Loss of jewelry, gold ornaments, silver articles and precious stones kept under lock & key

All the contents are covered on the market value of the items. This means that if there is a loss, the claim would be paid on the value of purchasing a similar new item, minus depreciation.

Health Insurance, India

It is said that a healthy mind resides in a healthy body. Hence it is very important to stay healthy. These days life is very fast and stressful. No matter how much you care one can always fall ill. Health treatment nowadays is very costly. More than the disease it is the cost of treatment that takes its toll. To get rid of health worries health / medical insurance is the answer. Health insurance policy not only covers expenses incurred during hospitalisation but also during the pre as well as post hospitalisation stages like money spent for conducting medical tests and buying medicines. The cover will be to the extent of the sum insured.

An added attraction of Mediclaim policies is the tax benefits which they attract under Section 80D. The maximum amount of deduction available under this section is Rs 10,000. In case of senior citizens, the maximum limit is Rs 15,000. Individuals also have the option of covering themselves for medical expenses by opting for the 'Critical Illness (CI)' rider available with life insurance policies.

Life insurance companies have their own list of critical illnesses as defined by them. In case of a CI rider, on the occurrence of a 'critical illness' during the policy tenure, an amount as proposed in the policy will be paid out to the individual. This is irrespective of the expenses incurred by the individual on hospitalisation, medicines and other such costs.

Health insurance companies are offering innovative products to their customers these days. The latest product in this line is 'cashless hospitalisation'. Here individuals do not have to pay for their hospital bills in case of hospitalisation; the insurance company settles the bill directly. But certain conditions like the hospital needs to have a tie-up with the insurance company, the documents need to be in order etc. have to be met.

Motor Insurance, India

Legally, no motor vehicle is allowed to be driven on the road without valid insurance. Hence, it is obligatory to get the vehicle insured.

Motor insurance policies cover against any loss or damage caused to the vehicle or its accessories due to the following natural and man made calamities.

Natural Calamities

Fire, explosion, self-ignition or lightning, earthquake, flood, typhoon, hurricane, storm, tempest, inundation, cyclone, hailstorm, frost, landslide, rockslide.

Man made Calamities

Burglary, theft, riot, strike, malicious act, accident by external means, terrorist activity, any damage in transit by road, rail, inland waterway, lift, elevator or air. Motor insurance provides compulsory personal accident cover for individual owners of the vehicle while driving. One can also opt for a personal accident cover for passengers and third party legal liability.

Third party legal liability protects against legal liability arising due to accidental damages. It includes any permanent injury / death of a person and damage caused to the property.

Travel Insurance, India

Travel and tourism is one of the most fast growing sectors around the world. With rise in standards of living, more and more people are embarking on journeys and exploring new places. Before going on a trip you need to address all your travel worries.

Travel insurance policy takes care of all your travel worries. It secures you and your loved ones in their sojourn abroad. Travel insurance plans offer host of benefits such as medical expenses, loss or delay of baggage or passport, personal accident, financial emergency assistance and hijack distress allowance.

Travel insurance plans cover expenses incurred due to delayed flight, cancellation of trip, and also take care of valued assets left at home.

3

GREATER CONVERGENCE AND COMMON CHALLENGES

INTRODUCITON

The forces of financial liberalisation, technological advances in elaborating and disseminating information and pricing complex financial instruments, and breakthroughs in financial risk management have made themselves felt across financial institutions and markets, across different types of financial institution and across national jurisdictions. By now we are all familiar with the broad contours of the powerful process of convergence that has been shaping the global financial industry over the past two decades.

First, the respective roles of capital markets and of financial institutions have been converging. Markets have made major inroads in the allocation of both funds and risks within the economy. They are now a key supplier of credit, they provide traditional insurance services, and they transfer risks across segments of the financial system, not least through derivatives. Initially, derivatives addressed market risk; now, the unfolding revolution is in instruments to manage credit risk. Crucially, in the process, the dividing lines between market traded and non-traded financial instruments and between insurance and other types of financial instruments that provide protection from specific risks have become increasingly blurred. Moreover, the relationship between markets and institutions has grown increasingly symbiotic.

On the one hand, institutions rely more and more on markets for their funding, for their investments and for the management of risks. On the other hand, markets rely more and more on institutions for their liquidity, drawing on market-making services and backstop credit lines.

Second, different types of financial institutions have been converging. This has been true even as the financial landscape has become more diverse. Many commercial banks have come to resemble investment banks as a growing proportion of their business has been channelled through the capital markets. And the growth of conglomerates that encompass both banking and insurance has eroded the long-standing barriers that had kept these two lines of business apart.

Third, financial arrangements across different national jurisdictions have been converging – a process that most of us know as "financial globalisation". As obstacles to capital flows, foreign establishment and the cross-border provision of financial services have come down, the pressure to adopt similar arrangements across countries has grown. These powerful forces of convergence have been mirrored in developments in risk management and in the prudential frameworks adopted by national authorities.

With risk management evolving from a side constraint on financial activity to a core function underpinning that activity, the similarities between the risks faced by different institutions have become increasingly apparent. In the process, the "language" barriers that used to separate the analysis of risks in different lines of business as well as in strands of academic thinking have slowly been breaking down. For example, a moment's reflection is sufficient to realise that Value-at-Risk measures that are common in banking and the stochastic asset-liability techniques that are common in insurance are, conceptually, the same sort of tool; they differ primarily with respect to the instruments included in the analysis and the horizon used for assessing risk.

This recognition has gone hand in hand with efforts to move towards a more integrated firm-wide approach to risk management. Across business lines, this means managing the same risk in the same way regardless of its location in an enterprise. Across different types of risk, it means developing a common metric for the aggregation of risks and for the calibration of economic capital. Clearly, even cutting-edge enterprises are a long way from achieving either objective. The broad direction, however, is unmistakable.

Likewise, prudential frameworks have been converging along different dimensions. Across national jurisdictions, it has become increasingly difficult to pursue country-specific solutions. International cooperation through the establishment of common standards, initially spearheaded in banking by the Basel Committee, has subsequently encompassed other regulatory groupings too, first securities regulators and then insurance supervisors. Across functional lines, the differences in approach have narrowed. For instance, capital adequacy, supervisory review of risk management processes, and enhanced public disclosures are all core elements of the prudential frameworks for both banking and insurance. The trend towards convergence has been strengthened by the establishment of "integrated supervisors" in a number of countries and, internationally, by the creation of the Joint Forum. The Forum has been performing a valuable role in identifying differences in prudential arrangements across sectors and in considering the ever larger set of issues of common interest across the different supervisory communities.

As an outside observer, I have always been struck by how much prudential authorities in banking and insurance can learn from each other, once the unfamiliarity with their respective approaches is overcome. Let me illustrate with a couple of examples. Insurance regulators have learned to focus on the risks to financial soundness that arise from the asset side of balance sheets, as opposed to focusing exclusively on the underwriting risks associated with insurance liabilities. For their part, banking supervisors are beginning to pay more attention to the adequacy of pricing policies in covering expected losses – which is a long-standing practice in insurance. I think that this is an area that will require much more attention in future. The message is that cross-fertilisation between the two communities of standard setters should be encouraged.

Against this background it is not surprising if the challenges faced by the two supervisory communities are increasingly shared ones. The financial reporting and macroprudential challenges that I highlighted at the beginning are the result of the same convergence forces that have been shaping the work of prudential authorities in other areas. And while I tend to place them primarily in the future, I do so simply because I feel that they will intensify in the years ahead. The future has in fact already started. Let me explore each challenge in turn.

THE FINANCIAL REPORTING CHALLENGE

Global financial markets – the epitome of the forces towards convergence -- naturally go hand in hand with global financial reporting practices. This is the rationale for the intense efforts that are under way to establish a common set of internationally accepted financial reporting standards (IFRS). There is a broad consensus over the importance that such standards can have for the proper functioning and stability of the financial system. Alongside core principles for prudential frameworks in banking and insurance, accounting standards are now part of the set of twelve standards that have been identified by the Financial Stability Forum as conducive to a robust financial infrastructure.

But it is one thing to agree on the importance of common financial reporting standards, and quite another to agree on a specific set. The development of international financial reporting standards has brought to the fore important differences in perspective between accounting standard setters on the one hand, and prudential authorities on the other, that will need to be reconciled. The stakes are high.

The first step in establishing a sound basis for this reconciliation is to understand the deep reasons for the differences of perspective. No doubt many factors are at play. After all, differences of opinion exist also within the two communities of standard setters. Even so, at the cost of some oversimplification, I would trace the reasons to differences in objectives and in approaches.

As regards objectives, accounting authorities have increasingly been seeking to establish "unbiased", or "true and fair", pictures of the financial condition of firms. This has meant departing somewhat from a time honoured accounting tradition that had leaned more towards conservative assessments of a firm's financial condition. As regards approach, accounting standard setters view the financial accounts as having to reflect the outcome of "past transactions and events". De facto, this has meant that in certain cases they have continued to stress the backward-looking elements of accounting statements of the financial condition of firms. By training, accountants and auditors are less at ease with risk concepts and risk measurement techniques. Consequently, they may on occasions set the bar for the verifiability of financial statements quite high when risk management questions are at play.

By contrast, the objective of financial supervisory authorities is to instill prudence in the behaviour of the firms they supervise. As a result, they are more naturally inclined to favour conservative valuations, often because these are seen as providing helpful safety cushions. As to approach, prudential authorities focus very much on prospective rather than past outcomes; risk is inevitably a forward-looking concept. And since the assessment of risks is the essence of their business, they may also be more disposed towards accepting verifiability thresholds that may appear insufficiently stringent in the eyes of their accounting counterparts. This is especially the case whenever the thresholds are seen as consistent with prudent risk management practices.

Let me clarify and illustrate. In banking, prudential authorities would like accounting standards to accommodate more forward-looking provisioning, since current rules are often seen as too backward-looking. Likewise, they would like to have greater flexibility to allow firms to macro-hedge their risks, a process that is rather foreign to their accounting counterparts because it runs counter to the principle of valuing assets and liabilities on an individual, as opposed to a portfolio, basis. In insurance, similar issues arise in the context of the valuation of renewal policies. Valuing them on the basis of an expected rate of renewal is common practice among actuaries, but not among accountants. The analogy with the valuation of core bank deposits is obvious.

What, then, about the way forward? Here, I think it is useful to distinguish between the long run goal, on the one hand, and the transition towards it, on the other.

As regards the long-run goal, we need to clearly keep in mind the different techniques and approaches that accountants and supervisors use, even though their ultimate goals are highly complementary. In other words, it seems natural for accounting to seek to portray the best approximation to an "unbiased" and comprehensive picture of the financial condition of the firm while prudential regulation seeks to instill the desired degree of prudence in its behaviour on the basis of that portrayal. Ideally, this would call for a unique set of valuations rather than one for accounting and another for prudential purposes.

And it would mean avoiding the expedient of setting safety cushions or buffers through conservative accounting per se. This would have the benefit of greater transparency, of avoiding the risk of unwittingly undermining either of the two objectives, and of facilitating convergence in accounting standards across both sectors and countries.

At the same time, it is essential that at all stages during the transition towards this long-run goal, the prudential authorities be in a position to redress any adverse implications that the needed changes in accounting standards may have for the safety and soundness of regulated financial intermediaries. In other words, the transition should be properly co-ordinated. For example, to the extent that an uneven recognition of fair value principles across asset categories might introduce artificial volatility in the accounts, prudential authorities should be in a position to counteract its impact on financial stability. While this issue has attracted considerable attention in banking, it is just as important, or perhaps even more important, in insurance.

Having said this, it is important to recognise two additional points about the final framework and the process towards it, respectively.

First, the portrayal of the financial condition of the firm should cover not just its profitability, cash flows and balance sheet, as it does today, but also its risk profile. This is an area where prudential authorities have taken the lead, by encouraging greater risk disclosures by regulated firms. Pillar 3 of the new Basel capital adequacy framework is the latest such example. The need for disclosure of risk information is beginning to be recognised by the accounting standard setters too; the IASB has launched a project in this area. The prudential standard setters are ideally placed to make major contributions to the development of such risk disclosure standards. And these efforts should be pursued vigorously.

Second, the contribution that prudential authorities can make to the development of standards goes well beyond providing more information on the risk profile of firms. We have all come to recognise that valuations and risk assessments are inextricably intertwined. Since economic agents care deeply about risk, the way current and prospective income streams are valued inevitably incorporates perceptions of risk as well as attitudes towards risk – commonly known as "risk appetite". It follows that prudential authorities can also bring precious value added to the rules for the compilation of traditional accounting information. Consistency between risk management practices and valuation is essential.

I am optimistic that, over time, we will make progress in the direction I have just outlined. Indeed, progress is being made as I speak. While much still needs to be done, the dialogue between prudential and accounting standard setters has become ever more intensive in recent years. I hope that it will become closer still in future, ideally through tighter institutional arrangements. Indeed, I am convinced that this dialogue will foster a greater understanding of the differences in perspective between accounting and prudential authorities, as well as greater convergence on the basis of shared perspectives and a "common language".

THE MACROPRUDENTIAL CHALLENGE

Next, what about the macroprudential challenge? Some of you may recall the keynote address delivered four years ago by my predecessor, Andrew Crockett. On that occasion, he argued that in order to improve safeguards against financial instability it was desirable to strengthen the macroprudential orientation of prudential frameworks, with respect to both the identification of vulnerabilities and the calibration of policy instruments. In practice, this would mean two things. First, shifting the focus somewhat from the safety and soundness of individual financial institutions to that of the financial system as a whole. Second, recognising more explicitly that while individual institutions may treat the underlying determinants of risk as independent of their actions, they can, collectively, have a first order effect on the determinants of risk themselves. For instance, lending booms can boost economic activity and asset prices to unsustainable levels, sowing the seeds of subsequent instability. Likewise, if a large number of financial market participants assume that markets will remain liquid even under collective selling pressure, they could be induced to overextend their position taking, thus generating the very pressure that would cause markets to become illiquid.

There are at least two reasons why a macroprudential perspective is important.

First, experience has shown that the financial crises that have the most serious costs for the economy tend to arise from shared exposures to risks -- typically macro risks -- rather than from individual failures that are due to institution-specific factors. This has been true both in banking and insurance. In banking, examples of these macro-financial risks include the banking crises in Nordic countries following financial liberalisation in the late 1980s, those in Japan in the early 1990s, and, more generally, those in several East Asian and

Latin American economies at various times over the past twenty years. In insurance, the recent Japanese experience is equally relevant.

In addition, the convergence observed within the financial industry has made such a system-wide perspective more compelling, as risks are more easily shifted across institutions and markets. For instance, in the period of global economic weakness that began in 2001, insurance companies fared far worse than banks precisely because banks had restrained their lending during the preceding boom. Instead, much corporate funding had been channelled through the capital markets, with insurance companies, for example, investing heavily in both bonds and equities. In addition, the possibility of shifting risks through the rapidly growing and less transparent credit derivatives markets has also played a role, although quantitatively a less important one so far.

By now, the importance of the macroprudential perspective as a complement to the more traditional microprudential focus is widely recognised. As a result, steps have been taken to put it into practice, both with respect to the identification of vulnerabilities and in the calibration of policy instruments.

As regards the task of identifying vulnerabilities in the financial system, macroprudential analysis is now routinely carried out in various guises. It is an integral part of Financial Sector Assessment Programs implemented jointly by the IMF and the World Bank. It is also a regular element of the monitoring exercises done in international fora, notably at the Financial Stability Forum and at the BIS-based Committee on the Global Financial System.

And it is more or less institutionalised in some national jurisdictions. Moreover, regular financial system monitoring has been complemented from time to time by more in-depth analysis of structural developments in the financial sector. The most obvious example is the set of studies done or under way on the impact of credit risk transfer instruments on the allocation of credit risk across the financial system, including by the Joint Forum.

As regards the calibration of prudential policy instruments, it is possible to find signs of a greater awareness of a macroprudential perspective in both banking and insurance. In banking, one such illustration is the various adjustments made to Basel II, partly with a view to addressing concerns about procyclicality. In insurance, one could point to the decision by the UK FSA in the autumn of 2002 to relax the stringency of stress tests so as to avoid the destabilising impact of cascading distress sales on the stock market.

I expect that these trends towards strengthening the macroprudential orientation will continue. My sense is that we are at the very beginning of the process. There is still much that we need to learn about the identification of system-wide vulnerabilities and the calibration of policy instruments.

And, to my mind, the basic principle that the framework should be designed to ensure that sound risk management practices lead to cushions that are built in good times so as to be run down, up to a point, in bad times, has not yet gained the currency that it deserves. I suspect that the merits of this principle would appear more obvious if fair value elements in accounting became more prevalent.

In achieving the shift towards a stronger macroprudential orientation, an even closer dialogue between central banks and prudential authorities will be especially helpful. After all, a macroprudential perspective is part of the DNA of central bankers, who can bring to the table the multifaceted expertise honed through the discharge of their monetary policy responsibilities. This dialogue has a long tradition, but I suspect that it will become even more important in future.

To conclude, let me just reiterate the key message. I have argued that the broadly-based process of convergence within the global financial system across markets, institutions and national jurisdictions puts a premium on a shared understanding of problems and on a shared formulation and implementation of solutions. I have illustrated this simple point with two challenges shared by banking and insurance supervisors, namely the need to ensure that accounting standards and prudential frameworks are mutually consistent, and the need to strengthen the macroprudential orientation of supervisory arrangements. In these, as in other areas, while much has been accomplished in recent years, there is clearly scope to intensify and broaden the dialogue within the financial policymaking community.

Indeed, in the balance of its own activities, the BIS has felt the convergence forces just as strongly as market participants and policymakers have. Since its inception, the hallmark of our institution has been to support the international dialogue within the policy community.

Over time, that function has been extended from central banks to prudential authorities, first in banking and more recently, albeit more indirectly, in insurance. Thus, we are replicating in the small the much larger shift in the world around us. Peering into the future, it is both my hope and expectation that the dialogue will continue to intensify and broaden. It would be a small but tangible sign that progress is being made.

LIFE INSURANCE CORPORATION OF INDIA

The Life Insurance Corporation of India (LICI) is the largest life insurance company in India; it is fully owned by the Government of India. It was founded in 1956.

Headquartered in Mumbai, which is considered the financial capital of India, the Life Insurance Corporation of India currently has 8 zonal Offices and 101 divisional offices located in different parts of India, at least 2048 branches located in different cities and towns of India along with satellite Offices attached to about some 50 Branches, and has a network of around one million and 200 thousand agents [1] for soliciting life insurance business from the public.

The Oriental Life Insurance Company, the first corporate entity in India offering life insurance cover was established in Calcutta in 1818 by Bipin Behari Dasgupta and others. Europeans in India were its primary target market, and it charged Indians heftier premiums. The Bombay Mutual Life Assurance Society, formed in 1870, was the first native insurance provider. Other insurance companies established in the pre-independence era included

- Bharat Insurance Company (1896)
- United India (1906)
- National Indian (1906)
- National Insurance (1906)
- Co-operative Assurance (1906)
- Hindustan Co-operative (1907)
- Indian Mercantile
- General Assurance
- Swadeshi Life (later Bombay Life)

The first 150 years were marked mostly by turbulent economic conditions. It witnessed, India's First War of Independence, adverse affects of the World War I and World War II on the economy of India, and in between them the period of world wide economic crises triggered by the Great depression. The first half of the 20th century also saw a heightened struggle for India's independence.

The aggregate effect of these events led to a high rate of bankruptcies and liquidation of life insurance companies in India. This had adversely affected the faith of the general public in the utility of obtaining life cover.

The LIFE INSURANCE Act and the Provident Fund Act were passed in 1912, providing the first regulatory mechanisms in the Life Insurance industry.

The Indian Insurance Companies Act of 1928 authorized the government to obtain statistical information from companies operating in both life and non-life insurance areas. The subsequent Insurance Act of 1938 brought stricter state control over an industry that had seen several financially unsound ventures fail. A bill was also introduced in the Legislative Assembly in 1944 to nationalize the insurance industry.

NATIONALIZATION

In 1955, parliamentarian Feroze Gandhi raised the matter of insurance fraud by owner's of private insurance companies. In the ensuing investigations, one of India's wealthiest businessmen, Ram Kishan Dalmia, owner of the Times of India newspaper, was sent to prison for two months.

Eventually, the Parliament of India passed the Life Insurance of India Act on 1956-06-19, and the Life Insurance Corporation of India was created on 1956-09-01, by consolidating the life insurance business of 245 private life insurers and other entities offering life insurance services. Nationalization of the life insurance business in India was a result of the Industrial Policy Resolution of 1956, which had created a policy framework for extending state control over at least seventeen sectors of the economy, including the life insurance. The company began operations with 5 zonal offices, 33 divisional offices and 212 branch offices.

Current Status

Over its existence of around 50 years, Life Insurance Corporation of India, which commanded a monopoly of soliciting and selling life insurance in India, created huge surpluses, and contributed around 7 % of India's GDP in 2006.

The Corporation, which started its business with around 300 offices, 5.6 million policies and a corpus of INR 459 million, has grown to 2,048 offices servicing around 180 million policies and a corpus of over INR 3.4 trillion.

The organization now comprises 2048 branches, 100 divisional offices and 8 zonal offices, and employs over 1 million agents. It also operates in 12 other countries, primarily to cater to the needs of Non Resident Indians.

With the change in the India's economic philosophy from the early 1990s, and the subsequent relaxation of state control over several sectors of the economy, the monopolistic position of the Life Insurance Corporation of India was diluted, and it has had to compete with a number of other corporate entities,

Indian as well as transnational Life Insurance brands.

In the fiscal year 2006-07 Life Insurance Corporation of India's number of policy holders are said to have crossed a whopping 200 million (fourth in terms of population of the countries of the world)

Subsidiaries

LIC owns the following subsidiaries:

- Life Insurance Corporation of India International: This is a joint venture offshore company promoted by LIC which commenced operations in July, 1989 with the objectives of offering US$ denomimated policies to cater to the insurance needs of NRIs and providing insurance services to holders of LIC policies currently residing in the Gulf. LIC International operates in all GCC countries.
- LIC Nepal: A joint venture company formed in 2001 with the Vishal Group of Industries, Nepal.
- LIC Lanka: A joint venture company formed in 2003 with the Bartleet Group of Companies, Sri Lanka.
- LIC Housing Finance: Incorporated in 19th June 1989, its main objective is to provide long term finance forconstruction or purchase of houses or apartments. It has a Dubai office.
    - LICHFL Care Homes: A wholly owned subsidiary of LIC Housing Finance, it builds and operates "Assisted Community Living Centres" for senior citizens.

Technology Usage

The insurance giant opted for internet services for all its subscribers and developed massive networking for own usage and internal governance. While the pros and cons of internal networking remains concealed within the officials and hidden for the common customers, the customer portal somehow fails to satisfy the 21st century customers. Apparently, low bandwidth, unwise web page hyper linking, illogical page set ups, all just contribute to the irritation of common net age customers.

The portal gives opportunity to register any policy to be tagged up with any one. As a matter of fact, if Mr. 'A' knows the policy number and premium value of certain policy 'X' of Mr. 'B,' 'A' can tag up 'X' with his own Profile in LICI portal and get all the details of the policy. Moreover, though the organization is officially known as Life Insurance Corporation of India, abbreviated, LICI, the portal welcomes a customer to LIC.

As a result of all these, online payment of premium through the site could not be a popular option for the customers. The site fails to show the details of all its recognized agents in its Agent locator section.

4

STRUCTURE OF INSURANCE

INTRODUCTION

Today, only one business, which affects all walks of life, is insurance business. That's why insurance industry occupies a very important place among financial services operative in the world. Owing to growing complexity of life, trade and commerce, individuals as well as business firms are turning to insurance to manage various risks. Therefore a proper knowledge of what insurance is and what purpose does it serve to individual or an organisation is therefore necessary.

Insurance is a mechanism that ensures an individual to thrive on adverse consequences by compensating the individual his/her loss financially. Every individual in this world is subject to unforeseen and uncalled for hazards or dangers, which may make him and his family vulnerable. At this place, only insurance helps him not only to survive but also recover his loss and continue his life in a normal manner, which would otherwise be unthinkable.

OBJECTIVES

After going through this lesson you should be able to:

- Explain the meaning of insurance
- Understand the nature and characteristics of insurance
- Discuss the need of getting insured and its benefits to individual and business firms

- Describe the types of insurance and their meaning
- List out the meanings of different terms used in the lesson
- Find out the new insurance products available in the market
- Discuss the historical background and the present state of insurance industry after liberalisation of insurance sector.

MEANING AND NATURE

The term insurance can be defined in financial as well as in legal terms. The financial definition deals with the funding or financial arrangement of the losses whereas the legal definition deals with provisions relating to legally enforceable contract.

Definition in Financial Sense

Insurance is a financial arrangement, which redistributes the costs of unexpected losses among the members of the pool. The pool is a collection of people facing common risks. All members contribute a fixed amount towards a pool called premium. In exchange for the premium payment, the person gets an assurance that a certain sum of money is to be paid to him on the happening of the event insured against. The assurance is that his loss will be made good. Thus, insurance involves the transfer of loss exposures to an insurance pool and the redistribution of losses among the members of the pool.

Definition in Legal Sense

Insurance can be defined as a contract between two parties by which one party undertakes to make good or indemnify any financial loss suffered by other party, in consideration of a sum of money, on the happening of a specified event e.g. fire, accident or death. We call the party agreeing to pay for the losses the insurer. We call the party whose loss makes the 'insurer' pay the claim the insured. We call the payment insured pays to the insurer the premium. We call the insurance contract a policy.

In the end we can sum up that insurance is a transfer of risk from the individual to the group and there is a sharing (pooling) of losses on some equitable basis such that fortuitous losses can be indemnified (paid).

Nature of Insurance

The insurance has the following characteristics, which are observed in case of life, marine, fire and general insurance. Sharing of risk-Insurance is a device to share the financial losses which might befall on an individual or his family on the happening of a specified event. The event may be death in case of life insurance, fire in fire insurance etc. If insured the loss arising from these events will be shared by all insured in the form of premium.

(1) Co-operative device-The most important feature of every insurance plan is the cooperation of large number of persons who, in effect, agree to share the financial loss arising due to a particular risk which is insured. An insurer would be unable to compensate all losses from his capital. So, by insuring a large number of persons, he is able to pay the amount of loss.

(2) Value of risk-The risk is evaluated before insuring to charge the amount of share of an insured, premium. There are several methods of evaluation of risks. If there is expectation of more risk, higher premium may be charged. So, the probability of loss is calculated at the time of insurance.

(4) Payment at contingency-The payment is made at a certain contingency insured. If the contingency occurs, payment is made. Since the life insurance contract is a contract of certainty, because the contingency, the death or the expiry of term, will certainly occur, the payment is certain. In other insurance contracts, the contingency is the fire or the marine perils etc., may or may not occur. So, if the contingency occurs, payment is made, otherwise no amount is given to the policy-holder.

(5) Amount of payment-The amount of payment depends upon the value of loss occurred due to the particular insured risk provided insurance is there up to that amount. In life insurance, the purpose is not to make good the financial loss suffered. The insurer promises to pay a fixed sum on the happening of an event. If the event or the contingency takes place, the payment falls due if the policy is valid and in force at the time of the event.

(6) Large number of insured persons-To spread the loss immediately, smoothly and cheaply, large number of persons should be insured. Large number of persons or property is insured to lower the cost of insurance and the amount of premium.

(7) Insurance is not a gambling-The insurance serves indirectly to increase the productivity of the community by eliminating worry and increasing initiative. The uncertainty is changed into certainty by insuring property and life because the insurer promises to pay a definite sum at damage or death.

From the company's point of view, the life insurance is essentially non-speculative; in fact, no other business operates with greater certainties. From the insured point of view, too, insurance is also the antithesis of gambling. Nothing is more uncertain than life and life insurance offers the only sure method of changing that uncertainty into certainty.

(8) Insurance is not charity-Charity is given without consideration but insurance is not possible without premium. It provides security and safety to an individual and to the security although it is a kind of business because in consideration of premium it guarantees the payment of loss. It is a profession because it provides adequate sources at the time of disasters only by charging a nominal premium for the service.

Purpose and Need

Beside things mentioned by you, let's discuss in detail the purpose and need of insurance. As we all know life is full of uncertainties and insurance is based on uncertainties and if there are no uncertainties about the occurrence of a disaster, the concept of insurance will cease to exist. If we all are able to predict the future dangers correctly then we can take a safeguard action to move out of the danger but problem is that we cannot predict death, disaster and danger.

All individuals as well as their tangible and intangible assets are exposed to all types of unforeseen risks. Thus insurance is done against such possible contingencies to save the owner and his family from all sorts of sufferings by making good the losses of the unfortunate few, through the help of the fortunate many, who were exposed to the same risk, but saved from the misfortune.

As insurance is a system of sharing risk that seems to be too great to be borne by one individual we can list out the benefits derived by individual and society from the insurance.

(1) Indemnifies loss-Insurance restores people to their former financial position as if no loss had occurred. It helps them to remain financially secure without running into debt after a loss. It also helps business firms to carry on their normal business operations without interruption even after the loss occurs.

(2) Reduces worry and fear-Insurance helps in reducing anxiety and fear before and after the loss occurs, as it is known that the insurance company will compensate the loss.

(3) Makes available funds for investment-Investments are the base of an economic development and mostly these investments are the result of savings. An insurance company is a major instrument for the mobilisation of the savings of people, which are thereafter canalised into investment for economic growth. Insurance provides

the continuity in trade and commerce, by covering the risks that could retard the economy and thereby indirectly helps the economy to grow.

(4) Provides employment to a large number of people-Insurance industry offers regular full time employment to a large number of people in the country. Besides them a number of agents, professionals etc. are also engaged by the industry to render professional services.

(5) Educates people about loss prevention-Insurance companies also engage themselves in educating people about loss prevention. In our country the GIC has created the loss prevention association of India to promote and propagate loss prevention.

(6) Insurance enhances credit worthiness-Insurance policies are often offered as collateral security for credit as well.

(7) Social benefits-Above all we derive social benefits when people with peaceful minds carry on their operations properly and in a better way. Thus insurance's contribution to the economy as a whole is valuable as it avoids economic hardships to people.

Principles of Insurance

Indemnity

A contract of insurance is a contract of indemnity. Indemnity means that the insured in case of loss against which the policy has been insured, shall be paid the actual amount of loss not exceeding the amount of the policy i.e. he shall be fully indemnified. The purpose of contract of insurance is to place the insured in the same financial position, as he was before the loss. Suppose, a person insured his factory for Rs.20 lakhs against fire, the factory is partially burnt and it is estimated that a sum of Rs.10 lakhs will be required to restore it to the original condition. The insurer is liable to pay Rs.10 lakhs only. The exceptions to the rule are found in Personal Accident policies, Agreed Value policies in marine insurance and

Valuables and reinstatement policies in Engineering insurance. These are also contracts of indemnity but by a special application of the principle, the amount of indemnity is decided at the time of entering into the contract itself.

In certain forms of insurance, the principle of indemnity is modified to apply. For example, in marine or fire insurance, sometimes, certain profit margin that would have earned in the absence of the event, is also included in the loss. Under life insurance, the insurer is required to pay the fixed amount in the event of death or on the expiry of the period of the policy.

Thus the contract of life insurance is not insurance as such but it is an assurance. This is due to the reason that life cannot be indemnified i.e. the life of a person cannot be valued in terms of money and therefore the question of compensation of actual loss does not arise. Thus a contract of life insurance is a contract of guarantee.

Utmost Good Faith

The doctrine of utmost good faith applies to all forms of insurance. Both parties of the insurance contract must be of the same mind at the time of contract. There should not be any fraud, non-disclosure or misrepresentation concerning the material facts. An insurance contract is a contract of absolute good faith where both parties of the contract must disclose all the material facts truly and fully as insurance shifts risk from one party to another. As in insurance insured knows more about the risks than the insurer, so there must be utmost good faith and mutual confidence between insured and insurer. For instance, if a person suffers from a serious invisible disease but does not disclose this fact while getting his life insured, the insurance company can avoid the contract.

Similarly the insurer must exercise the same good faith in disclosing the scope of the insurance, which he is prepared to grant. Breach of good faith renders the contract voidable ab initio at the discretion of the aggrieved party. A material fact is a fact which would influence the mind of an insurer in deciding whether he should accept the risk, on what terms and what premium he should charge. The utmost good faith says that all material facts should be disclosed in true and full form. It means that the facts should be disclosed in that form in which they really exist. There should no false statement and no half-truth nor any silence on the material facts. What is a material fact depends upon the circumstances of the particular case.

Insurable Interest

For an insurance contract to be valid, the insured must have an insurable interest in the subject matter of insurance. It means that the insured must have an actual pecuniary interest. The insured must be so situated with regard to the thing insured that he would have benefit by its existence and loss from its destruction. For instance, a person has insurable interest in his life or in the life of the spouse but he has no insurable interest in the life of a stranger.

The owner of a building has absolute insurance interest. If this building is financed by banks then financiers too have their interest in the property but is limited to the extent of their financial commitment only.

The insurable interest must exist both at the time of the proposal and at the time of claims but in case of life insurance, insurable interest must exist only when the policy is taken.

The essentials of a valid insurable interest are the following:

(a) There must be a subject matter to be insured.

(b) The insured should have monetary relationship with the subject matter.

(c) The relationship between the insured and the subject matter should be recognised by law i.e. there should not be any illegal relationship between the insured and the subject matter.

(d) The financial relationship between the insured and the subject matter should be such that the insured is financially benefited by its existence or survival and will suffer economic loss at the destruction or death of the subject matter.

The subject matter is life in life insurance, property and goods in property insurance, liability and adventure in general insurance. Insurable interest is essentially a pecuniary interest, no emotional or sentimental loss, like an expectation or an anxiety, could be the ground of the insurable interest.

Proximate Cause

The rule of proximate cause says that the cause of the loss must be proximate or immediate and not remote. If the proximate cause of the loss is a risk insured against, the insured can recover. If the risk insured is the outcome of a remote cause, which is not insured against, then the insurer is not bound to pay compensation. Proximate cause means the active efficient cause that sets in motion a chain of events, which brings about a result, without intervention of any force started and working actively from a new and independent source. That means proximate cause is the cause which in a natural and unbroken series of events is responsible for a loss or damage.

If there is a single cause of the loss, the cause will be proximate cause and if the cause of loss was insured, insurer will have to indemnify the loss. When a loss has been brought about by two or more causes, the question arises as to which is the proximate cause. If the causes occurred in form of chain, they have to be observed seriously. For the policy to cover the loss must have an insured peril must occur in the chain of causation that links the proximate cause with the loss. The proximate cause is not necessarily, the cause that was nearest to the damage either in time or in place, but is rather the cause that was actually responsible for loss.

Subrogation

The doctrine of subrogation is a corollary to the principle of indemnity and applies only to fire and marine insurance. According to it, when an insured has received full indemnity in respect of his loss, all rights and remedies which he has against third person will pass on to the insurer.

The insurer's right of subrogation arises only when he has paid for the loss and this right extend only to the rights and remedies available to the insured in respect of the thing to which the contract of insurance relates.

If the insured is in a position to recover the loss in full or in part from a third party due to whose negligence the loss may have been occurred, his right of recovery is subrogated (substituted) to the insurer on settlement of the claim.

The insurers, thereafter, can recover the claim from the third party or in case the lost property is recovered or the damaged property fetches any value, the insurer will be its owner. Suppose, a house is insured for Rs.2 lakhs against fire, the house is damaged by fire and the insurer pays the full value of Rs.2 lakhs to the insured. Later on the damaged house is sold for Rs.20, 000. The insurer is entitled to receive the sum of Rs.20, 000.

Contribution

When an insured obtains more than one policy on one risk, the principle of contribution comes into play. The aim of contribution is to distribute the actual amount of loss among the different insurers who are liable for the same risk under different policies in respect of the same subject matter.

That means the insured may effect more than policy to cover the same risk, he/she cannot recover in total more than a full indemnity (sum insured). In other words, the right of contribution arises when (a) there are different policies which relate to the same subject matter (b) the policies cover the same peril which caused the loss (c) all the policies are in force at the time of the loss and (d) one of the insurers has paid to the insured more than his share of the loss. However, the principle of contribution does not apply to life insurance.

Mitigation of Loss

In the event of a mishap, the insured must take all possible steps to mitigate or minimise the loss to the subject matter of insurance. He should act in the same manner in which he would have acted in the absence of the insurance cover. This means that it is the duty of the insured to make a reasonable effort and take all available precautions to save the insured property.

Warranties

There are certain conditions and promises in the insurance contract which are called warranties. Warranties which are mentioned in the policy are called express warranties. There are certain warranties which are not mentioned in the policy.

These warranties are called implied warranties. Warranties, which are answers to the question, are called affirmative warranties. The warranties fulfilling certain conditions or promises are called promissory warranties.

Warranty is the very important condition in the insurance contract which is to be fulfilled by the insured. On breach of warranty the insurer becomes free from his liability. Therefore insured must have to fulfil the condition and promises during the insurance contract whether it is important or not in connection with the risk.

If warranties are not followed, the other party may cancel the contract whether risk has occurred or not. However, when the warranty is declared illegal and there is no reverse effect on the contract, the warranty can be waived.

Types of Insurance

The insurance can be divided from two angles: from business point of view and from the risk point of view.

Business Point of View

The insurance from business point of view can be categorised into:

(1) Life Insurance,

(2) General Insurance, and

(3) Social Insurance.

Life Insurance

Life Insurance is different from other insurance in the sense that the subject matter of insurance is life of human being. The insurer will pay the fixed amount of insurance at the death or at the expiry of certain period. At present, life insurance enjoys maximum scope because each and every person requires the insurance. This insurance provides protection to the family at the premature death or gives adequate amount at the old age when earning capacities are reduced. Types of insurance plans offered in our country:

- Term assurance plans
- Whole life plans
- Endowment assurance plans
- Assurances for children
- Family income policy
- Life annuity Joint life assurance
- Pension plans
- Unit linked plan
- Policy for maintenance of handicapped dependent
- Endowment policies with health insurance benefits

General Insurance

The general insurance includes property insurance, liability insurance and other forms of insurance. Fire and marine insurance comes under property insurance. Liability insurance includes motor, theft, fidelity and machine insurances to a certain extent. The strictest form of liability insurance is fidelity insurance whereby the insurer compensates the loss to the insured when he is under the liability of payment to the third party. Types of insurance policies available are:

- Health insurance
- Medi-claim policy
- Personal accident policy

- Group insurance policy
- Automobile insurance
- Worker's compensation
- Liability insurance
- Aviation insurance
- Business insurance
- Fire insurance policy
- Travel insurance policy

Social Insurance

The social insurance is to provide protection to the weaker sections of the society who are unable to pay the premium for adequate insurance. Pension plan, disability benefits, unemployment benefits, sickness insurance and industrial insurance are the various forms of social insurance.

Risk Point of View

Insurance can be divided into property, liability and other forms of insurance.

Property Insurance

Under the property insurance property of a person is insured against a certain specified risks. The risk may be fire or marine perils, theft of property or goods, damage to property at accident. Examples of this are:

- Home insurance
- Business insurance
- Commercial insurance

Marine Insurance

Marine insurance provides protection against loss of marine perils. The marine perils are collision with rock, or ship attacks by enemies, fire and capture by pirates etc. These perils cause damage, destruction or disappearance of the ship and cargo and non-payment of freight. So, marine insurance insures ship (Hull), cargo and freight. Types of policies are:

- Voyage policies
- Time policies
- Valued policies
- Hull insurance
- Cargo insurance
- Freight insurance

Fire Insurance

Fire insurance covers risks of fire. In thc absence of fire insurance, the fire waste will increase not only to the individual but to the society as well. With the help of fire insurance, the losses, arising due to fire are compensated and the society is not losing much. The individual is protected from such losses and his property or business or industry will remain in the same position in which it was before the loss. The fire insurance does not protect only losses but it provides certain consequential losses also. Policies available in this insurance are:

- Consequential loss policy
- Comprehensive policy
- Valued policy
- Valuable policy
- Floating policy
- Average policy

Miscellaneous Insurance

The property, goods, machine, furniture, automobile, valuable goods etc., can be insured against the damage or destruction due to accident or disappearance due to theft. There are different forms of insurances for each type of the said property whereby not only property insurance exists but liability insurance and personal injuries are also insured. Miscellaneous insurance covers:

- Motor
- Disability
- Engineering and aviation risks
- Credit insurance
- Construction risks
- Money insurance
- Burglary and theft insurance
- All risks insurance

Liability Insurance

The general insurance also includes liability insurance whereby the insurer is liable to pay the damage of property or to compensate the loss of personal injury or death. The examples of this type of insurance are fidelity insurance, automobile insurance and machine insurance. Examples are:

- Third party insurance
- Employees insurance
- Reinsurance

Other Forms

Besides the property and liability insurances, there are certain other insurances, which are included under general insurance. The examples of such insures are export credit insurances, state employees insurance, etc. whereby the insurer guarantees to pay certain amount at the happening of certain events. Examples are:

- Fiduciary insurance
- Credit insurance
- Privilege insurance

INSURANCE PRODUCTS AND STATE OF INSURANCE INDUSTRY IN INDIA

Terminology

- *Loss* – Loss means being without something which is previously possessed.

- *Total Loss* – A total loss implies that the subject matter insured is fully destroyed and is totally lost to its owner.
- *Actual Loss* – In actual loss subject matter is completely destroyed or so damaged that it ceases to be a thing of the kind insured like complete destruction of cargo by fire.
- *Constructive total loss* – In case of constructive total loss the ship or cargo insured is not completely destroyed but is so badly damaged that the cost of repair or recovery would be greater than the value of the property saved.
- *Partial loss* – A partial loss occurs when the subject matter is partially destroyed or damaged.
- *General Average* – General average refers to the sacrifice made during extreme circumstances for the safety of the ship and the cargo. This loss has to be borne by all the parties who have an interest in the marine adventure.
- *Particular Average* – Particular average may be defined as a loss arising from damage accidentally caused by the perils insured against. Such a loss is borne by the underwriter who insured the object damaged.
- *Peril* – A peril is defined as the cause of the loss. Examples of perils include fires, tornadoes, heart attacks and criminal acts. Insurance policies provide financial protection against losses caused by perils.
- *Hazards* – hazards are conditions that increase either the frequency or the severity of losses.
- *Warranties* – A warranty is that by which the assured undertakes that some particular thing shall or shall not be done, or that some conditions shall be fulfilled, or whereby he affirms or negatives the existence of a particular state of facts.
- *Reinsurance* – It is an arrangement whereby an original insurer who has insured a risk insures a part of that risk again with another insurer, that means reinsures a part of the risk in order to diminish his liability.

- *Jettison* – Jettison means voluntary throwing away of the cargo or part of a vessel's equipment for the lightening or relieving the ship for common safety. The aim of the intentional throwing away of the goods or property is to relieve the vessel from some imminent peril.
- *Enemies* – The ships belonging to the enemy may cause loss to the insured and is re-underwritten by the marine policy. This policy extends to all the persons of the enemy country and to their hostile acts provided such acts from part of the enemy actions.
- *Agent*–A licensed person or organization authorized to sell insurance by or on behalf of an insurance company.
- *Broker* – A licensed person or organization paid by you to look for insurance on your behalf
- *Burglary* – Coverage against loss as a result of forced entry into premises.
- *Claim* – Notice to an insurer that under the terms of a policy, a loss maybe covered Disability Insurance-Health insurance that provides income payments to the insured wage earner when income is interrupted or terminated because of illness, sickness, or accident.
- *Grace Period* – A period (usually 31 days) after the premium due date, during which an overdue premium may be paid without penalty. The policy remains in force throughout this period.
- *Material Misrepresentation* – The policyholder / applicant makes a false statement of any material (important) fact on his/her application. For instance, the policyholder provides false information regarding the location where the vehicle is garaged.
- *Policy* – The written contract of insurance.
- *Premium* – The amount of money an insurance company charges for insurance coverage.
- *Underwriting* – The process of selecting applicants for insurance and classifying them according to their degrees

of insurability so that the appropriate premium rates may be charged. The process includes rejection of unacceptable risks. Workers Compensation Insurance-Coverage providing four types of benefits (medical care, death, disability, and rehabilitation) for employee job-related injuries or diseases as a matter of right (without regard to fault).

New Insurance Products

Some of the new policies are:

(1) Policies under LIC Mutual Fund – LIC launched its Mutual Fund with promise to the investors to provide high returns along with safety and security of investments. LIC Mutual Fund came up with 5 schemes which provide distinct benefits to various cross sections of investors. The names of scheme are:

- Dhanashree 1989
- Dhan 80 cc(1)
- Dhanavarsha
- Dhanaraksha 1989
- Dhanavridhi 1989

(2) Jeevan Akshay – In return for purchase price paid by the purchaser a monthly pension will be paid during the lifetime of the purchaser of the pension. On the death of the pensioner, the original amount invested by the employee along with an additional bonus will be returned to the nominee or his legal heirs.

(3) Jeevan Dhara – The payment of annuities in respect of policies under Jeevan Dhara has to start one month after the completion of the deferment period.

(4) Jeevan Kishor – Children between the ages of 1(last birthday) and 12(last birthday) are eligible to be proposed for insurance under this plan.

(5) Jeevan Chhaya – Couples having a child of age less than one year can avail of this plan, in order to ensure

that an adequate financial provision is made for the higher education of the child. The child should not have completed one year of age on the date of the registration. Either father or mother or each one of them individually can take policies under this plan.

(6) Jeevan Suraksha – This policy enables individuals to provide for retirement income from a chosen date. The policy is with life cover but can be taken without life cover under certain conditions.

(7) Rural insurance – The policies offered under this scheme are:

Personal Insurance

(a) Janta Personal Accident (Individual)

(b) Janta Personal Accident (Group)

(c) Gramin Personal Accident

Property Insurance

(a) Agricultural Pumpset

(b) Animal Driven Carts Insurance

(c) Hut Insurance

(d) Gober Gas Insurance

(e) New Well Insurance

Cattle and Livestock Insurance

(a) Cattle Insurance

(b) Sheep and Goat Insurance

(c) Camel Insurance

(d) Horse Insurance

Poultry Insurance

(a) Duck Insurance

(b) Poultry Insurance Master Policy

(8) Insurance of Species

(9) Package Insurance

(10) Crop Insurance

(11) Medi-claim Hospitalisation and

Domiciliary Hospitalisation Insurance

(12) Overseas Medi-claim Policy

(13) Student's Safety Insurance

(14) Unborn Child Welfare Insurance

(15) Cancer Medical Expenses Policy

(16) Boiler and Pressure Plant Insurance

(17) Machinery Insurance

(18) Cold Storage Insurance

(19) Baggage Insurance

(20) Shopkeeper's Insurance

(21) All Risks Cover Insurance

(22) Social Security Scheme

(23) Wedding Insurance

(24) Kidnap and ransom Insurance

(25) Travel Insurance.

Composition of Authority

The Authority shall consist of the following members, namely:

(a) a Chairperson;

(b) not more than five whole-time members;

(c) not more than four part-time members, to be appointed by the Central Government from amongst persons of ability, integrity and standing who have knowledge or experience in life insurance, general insurance, actuarial science, finance, economics, law, accountancy, administration or any other discipline which would, in the opinion of the Central Government, be useful to the Authority:

The Central Government while appointing the Chairperson and the whole-time members must ensure that at least one person each is a person having knowledge or experience in life insurance, general insurance or actuarial science respectively.

Tenure of office of Chairperson and other members The Chairperson and every other whole-time member shall hold office for a term of five years from the date on which he enters upon his office and shall be eligible for reappointment: However, no person shall hold office as such Chairperson after he has attained the age of sixty-five years and no person shall hold office as such whole-time member after he has attained the age of sixty-two years.

A part-time member shall hold office for a term not exceeding five years from the date on which he enters upon his office.

A member may:-

(a) relinquish his office by giving in writing to the Central Government notice of not less than three months; or be removed from his office in accordance with the following provisions.

Removal from Office

The Central Government may remove from office any member who:-

(a) is, or at any time has been, adjudged as insolvent;

(b) has become physically or mentally incapable of acting as a member;

(c) has been convicted of any offence which, in the opinion of the Central Government, involves moral turpitude;

(d) has acquired such financial or other interest as is likely to affect prejudicially his functions as a member;

(e) has so abused his position as to render his continuation in office detrimental to the public interest.

No such member shall be removed under clause (d) or clause (e) unless he has been given a reasonable opportunity of being heard in the matter. Salary and allowances of Chairperson and members

The salary and allowances payable to, and other terms and conditions of service of, the members other than part-time members shall be such as may be prescribed.

The part-time members shall receive such allowances as may be prescribed. The salary, allowances and other conditions of service of a member shall not be varied to his disadvantage after appointment.

Bar on Future Employment of Members

The Chairperson and the whole-time members shall not, for a period of two years from the date on which they cease to hold office as such, except with the previous approval of the Central Government, accept:-

(a) any employment either under the Central Government or under any State Government; or

(b) any appointment in any company in the Insurance sector.

Administrative powers of Chairperson

The Chairperson shall have the powers of general superintendence and direction in respect of all administrative matters of the Authority.

Meeting of Authority

The Authority shall meet at such times and places, and shall observe such rules and procedures in regard to transaction of business at its meetings (including quorum at such meetings) as may be determined by regulations. The Chairperson, or if for any reason he is unable to attend a meeting of the Authority, any other member chosen by the members present from amongst themselves at the meeting shall preside at the meeting. All questions which come up before any meeting of the Authority shall be decided by a majority vote of the members present and voting, and in the event of equality of votes, the Chairperson, or in his absence, the person presiding shall have a second or casting vote. The Authority may make regulations for the transaction of business at its meetings.

Vacancies, etc., not to Invalidate Proceedings of Authority

No Act or proceeding of the Authority shall be invalid merely by reason of:-

(a) any vacancy in, or any defect in the constitution of, the Authority;

(b) any defect in the appointment of a person acting as a member of the Authority;

(c) any irregularity in the procedure of the Authority not affecting the merits of the case.

Officers and Employees of Authority

The Authority may appoint officers and such other employees, as it considers necessary for the efficient discharge of its functions under this Act. The terms and other conditions of service of officers and other employees of the Authority shall be governed by regulations made under this Act.

Transfer of Assets, Liabilities, etc, of the Interim Insurance Regulatory

Authority will be transferred to the Authority on the appointed day.

All suits and other legal proceedings instituted or which could have been instituted by or against the Interim Insurance Regulatory Authority immediately before that day may be continued or may be instituted by or against the Authority.

Duties, Powers and Functions of Authority

Subject to the provisions of this Act and any other law for the time being in force, the Authority has the duty to regulate, promote and ensure orderly growth of the insurance business and re-insurance business. The powers and functions of the Authority include:-

(a) to issue to the applicant a certificate of registration, to renew, modify, withdraw, suspend or cancel such registration

(b) protection of the interests of the policy-holders in matters concerning assigning of policy, nomination by policy-holders, insurable interest, settlement of insurance claim, surrender value of policy, and other terms and conditions of contracts of insurance

(c) specifying requisite qualifications code of conduct and practical training for intermediary or insurance intermediaries and agents

(d) specifying the code of conduct for surveyors and loss assessors

(e) promoting efficiency in the conduct of insurance business

(f) promoting and regulating professional organizations connected with the insurance and reinsurance business

(g) levying fees and other charges for carrying out the purposes of this Act

(h) calling for information from, undertaking inspection of, conducting enquiries and investigations including audit of the insurers, intermediaries, insurance intermediaries and other organizations connected with the insurance business

(i) control and regulation of the rates, advantages, terms and conditions that may be offered by insurers in respect of general insurance business not so controlled and regulated by the Tariff Advisory Committee under section 64U of the Insurance Act, 1938

(j) prescribing the form and manner in which books of account shall be maintained and statement of accounts will be rendered by insurers and other insurance intermediaries

(k) Regulating investment of funds by insurance companies

(l) regulating maintenance of margin of solvency

(m) adjudication of disputes between insurers and intermediaries or insurance intermediaries

(n) supervising the functioning of the Tariff Advisory Committee

(o) specifying the percentage of premium income of the insurer to finance schemes for promoting and regulating professional organizations

(p) specifying the percentage of life insurance business and general insurance business to be undertaken by the insurer in the rural or social sector

(q) exercising such other powers as may be prescribed

Finance, Accounts and Audit

Grants by Central Government

The Central Government may, after due appropriation made by the Parliament by law in this behalf, make to the Authority grants of such sums of money as the Government may think fit for being utilized for the purposes of this Act.

Fund

A Fund to be called "The Insurance Regulatory and Development Authority Fund" is to be established and the following sums will be credited thereto:-

(a) all Government grants, fees and charges received by the Authority

(b) all sums received by the Authority from such other source as may be decided upon by the Central Government

(c) the percentage of prescribed income received from the insurer.

The Fund shall be applied for meeting the following expenses:-

(a) the salaries, allowances and other remuneration of the members, officers and other employees of the Authority

(b) the other expenses of the Authority in connection with the discharge of its functions and for the purposes of this Act.

Accounts and Audit

The Authority shall maintain proper accounts and other relevant records and prepare an annual statement of accounts in such form as may be prescribed by the Central Government in consultation with the Comptroller and Auditor General of India. The accounts of the Authority shall be audited by the Comptroller and Auditor General of India at such intervals as may be specified by him and any expenditure incurred in connection with such audit shall be payable by the Authority to the Comptroller and Auditor General of India. The Comptroller and Auditor-General of India and other person appointed by him in connection with the audit of the accounts of the Authority shall have the same rights and privileges and authority in connection with such audit as the Comptroller and Auditor General generally has in connection with the audit of the Government accounts and, in particular, shall have the right to demand the production of books, accounts, connected vouchers and other documents and papers and to inspect any of the officers of the Authority. The accounts of the Authority as certified by the Comptroller and Auditor General of India or any other person appointed by him in this behalf together with the audit report thereon shall be forwarded annually to the Central Government and that Government shall cause the same to be laid before each House of Parliament.

Powers of Central Government

The Authority shall, in exercise of its powers or the performance of its functions under this Act, be bound by such directions on questions of policy, other than those relating to technical and administrative matters, as the Central Government may give in writing to it from time to time However, Authority must, as far as practicable, be given an opportunity to express its views before any such direction is given. The decision of the Central Government, whether a question is one of policy or not, shall be final. Power of Central Government to supersede Authority If at any time the Central Government is of the opinion:-

(a) that, on account of circumstances beyond the control of the Authority, it is unable to discharge the functions or perform the duties imposed on it by or under the provisions of this Act: or

(b) that the Authority has persistently defaulted in complying with any direction given by the Central Government under this Act or in the discharge of the functions or performance of the duties imposed on it by or under the provisions of this Act and as a result of such default the financial position of the Authority or the administration of the Authority has suffered; or

(c) that circumstances exist which render in necessary in the public interest so to do, the Central Government may, by notification and for reasons to be specified therein, supersede the Authority for such period, not exceeding six months, as may be specified in the notification and appoint a person to be the Controller of Insurance. However, before issuing any such notification, the Central Government shall give a reasonable opportunity to the Authority to make representations against the proposed supersession and shall consider the representations, if any, of the Authority.

Upon the publication of such notification superseding the Authority:-

(a) the Chairperson and other members shall, as from the date of supersession, vacate their offices as such;

(b) all the powers, functions and duties which may, by or under the provisions of this Act, be exercised or discharged by or on behalf of the Authority shall, until the Authority is reconstituted, be exercised and discharged by the Controller of Insurance; and

(c) all properties owned or controlled by the Authority shall, until the Authority is reconstituted vest in the Central Government.

On or before the expiration of the period of supersession specified in such a notification, the Central Government shall reconstitute the Authority by a fresh appointment of its Chairperson and other members and in such case any person who had vacated his office under the notification shall not be deemed disqualified for reappointment.

The Central Government shall cause a copy of the notification issued and a full report of any action taken under this section and the circumstances leading to such action to be laid before each House of Parliament at the earliest.

Furnishing of Eeturns, etc., to the Central Government

The Authority must furnish to the Central Government at such time and in such form and manner as may be prescribed, or as the Central Government may direct, such returns and statements and such particulars in regard to any proposed or existing programme for the promotion and development of the insurance industry as the Central Government may, from time to time, require.

The Authority must, within nine months after the close of each financial year, submit to the Central Government a report giving a true and full account of its activities including the activities for promotion and development of the insurance business during the previous financial year. Copies of the reports must be laid, as soon as may be after they are received, before each House of Parliament.

Chairperson, members, officers and employees of Authority to be public servants. The Chairperson, members, officers and other employees of the Authority shall be deemed, when acting or purporting to act in pursuance of any of the provisions of this Act, to be public servants within the meaning of section 21 of the Indian Penal Code.

Protection of Action taken in Good Faith

No suit, prosecution or other legal proceedings shall lie against the Central Government or any officer of the Central Government or any member, officer or other employee of the Authority for anything which is in good faith done or intended to be done under this Act or the rules or regulations made there under. However, nothing in this Act exempts any person from any suit or other proceedings which might, apart from this Act, be brought against him.

Delegation of Powers

The Authority may, by general or special order in writing, delegate to the Chairperson or any other member or officer of the Authority, subject to such conditions, if any, as may be specified in the order such of its powers and functions under this Act as it may deem necessary. The Authority may, by a general or special order in writing, also form Committees of the members and delegate to them the powers and functions of the Authority as may be specified by the regulations.

Power to make Rules

The Central Government may, by notification, make rules for carrying out the purposes of this Act. Such rules may provide for all or any of the following matters, namely:-

(a) the salary and allowances payable to and other conditions of service of the members other than part-time members

(b) the allowances to be paid to the part-time members

(c) such other powers that may be performed by the Authority

(d) the form of annual statement of accounts to be prepared by the Authority

(e) the time at, the form and the manner in which returns and statements and particulars are to be furnished to the Central Government

(f) the matters on which the Insurance Advisory Committee shall advise the authority

(g) any other matter which is to be, or may be, prescribed, or in respect of which provision is to be or may be made by rules.

Establishment of Insurance Advisory Committee

The Authority may, by notification, establish with effect from such date as it may specify in such notification, a Committee to be known as the Insurance Advisory Committee. The Insurance Advisory Committee shall consist of not more than twenty-five members excluding ex officio members to represent the interests of commerce, industry, transport, agriculture, consumer fora, surveyors, agents, intermediaries, organizations engaged in safety and loss prevention, research bodies and employees' association in the insurance sector.

The Chairperson and the members of the Authority shall be the ex officio Chairperson and ex officio members of the Insurance Advisory Committee. The objects of the Insurance Advisory committee shall be to advise the Authority on matters relating to the making of the regulations. The Insurance Advisory Committee may advise the Authority on such other matters as may be prescribed.

Capital Requirements

Requirement as to Capital

No insurer carrying on the business of life insurance, general insurance, or reinsurance in India on or after the commencement of the Insurance Regulatory and Development Authority Act, 1999, shall be registered unless he has:-

1. a paid-up equity capital of rupees one hundred crores, in case of a person carrying on the business of life insurance or general insurance; or
2. a paid-up equity capital of rupees two hundred crores, in case of a person carrying on exclusively the business as a reinsurer:

In determining the paid-up equity capital specified under clause (i) or clause (ii), the deposit to be made under section

7 and any preliminary expenses incurred in the formation and registration of the company shall be excluded: An insurer carrying on business of life insurance, general insurance or reinsurance in India before the commencement of the Insurance Regulatory and Development Authority Act, 1999 and who is required to be registered under this Act, shall have a paid-up equity capital in accordance with clause (i) and clause (ii), as the case may be, within six months of the commencement of that Act.

Where, the nominal value of the shares intended to be transferred by any individual, firm, group, constituents of a group, or body corporate under the same management, jointly or severally exceeds one per cent. Of paid up capital of the insurer, previous approval of the Authority must be obtained for the transfer.

Explanation.-For the purpose of this sub-clause, the expressions "group" and "same management", shall have the same meanings respectively assigned to them in the Monopolies and Restrictive Trade Practices Act, 1969.

The following sections have been inserted:-

Provisions of investment of funds outside India.

No insurer shall directly or indirectly invest outside India, the funds of the policyholders.

Manner and Conditions of Investment

The Authority may, in the interests of the policyholders, specify by regulations made by the Authority, the time, manner and other conditions of investment of assets to be held by an insurer for the purposes of this Act.

The Authority may, after taking into account the nature of business and to protect the interests of the policyholders, issue to an insurer the directions relating to the time, manner, and other conditions of investment of assets to be held by him. However, no directions shall be issued unless the insurer concerned has been given a reasonable opportunity of being heard.

Insurance Business in Rural or Social Sector

Every insurer shall, after the commencement of the Insurance Regulatory and Development Authority Act, 1999, undertake such percentages of life insurance business and general insurance business in the rural or social sector, as may be specified, in the Official Gazette by the Authority, in this behalf.

Miscellaneous Provisions

Penalty for default in complying with, or act in contravention of, this Act. lf any person, who is required under this Act, or rules or regulations made there under,-

(a) to furnish any document, statement, account, return or report to the Authority, fail to furnish the same; or

(b) to comply with the directions, fails to comply with such directions;

(c) to maintain solvency margin, fails to maintain such solvency margin;

(d) to comply with the directions on the insurance treaties, fails to comply with sue directions on the insurance treaties, he shall be liable to a penalty not exceeding five lakhs rupees for each such failure and punishable with fine.

lf a person makes a statement, or furnishes any document, statement, account, return or report which is false and which he either knows or believes to be false or does not believe to be true,

(a) he shall be liable to a penalty not exceeding five lakhs rupees for each such failure; and

(b) he shall be punishable with imprisonment which may extend to three years or with fine for each such failure.

If any director, managing director, manager or to~ officer or employees of an insurer wrongfully obtains possession of any property or wrongfully applies to any purpose of the Act, he shall be liable to a penalty not exceeding two lakhs rupees for each such failure.

Offences by companies, Where any offence under this Act has been committed by a company, every person who, at the time the offence was committed, was in charge of, and was responsible to, the Company for the conduct of the business of the company as well as the company shall be deemed to be guilty of the offence and shall be liable to be proceeded against and punished accordingly: Nothing contained in this sub-section shall render any such person liable to any punishment, if he proves that the offence was committed without his knowledge or that he had exercised all due diligence to prevent the commission of such offence. Where any offence under this Act has been committed by a company and it is proved that the offence has been committed with the consent or connivance of, or is attributable to any neglect on the part of, any director, manager, secretary or other officer of the company, such director, manager, secretary or other officer shall be deemed to be guilty of that offence and shall be liable to be proceeded against and punished accordingly.

Explanation: For the purposes of this section,-

(a) "company" means any body corporate, and includes a firm, an association of person or a body of individuals whether incorporated or not; and

(b) "director", in relation to-

   (i) a firm means a partner in the firm;

   (ii) an association of persons or a body of individuals, means any-member controlling the affairs thereof.

Power of Authority to make regulations.

The Authority may, by notification in the Official Gazette, make regulations consistent with this Act and the rules made there under, to carry out the provisions of this Act.

AGENCY LAW

At times all of us act as principals and agents. If I my friend ask me to deposit his water bill, then he is acting as principal and I am as agent. Agency Law is contained in Chapter X

{Secs182 to 238} of the Indian Contact Act 1872. "Agent" and "principal": An "agent" is a person employed to do any act for another, or to represent another in dealings with third persons. The person for whom such act is done, or represented, is called the "principal". {sec182}.

Who may employ agent: Any person who is of the age of majority according to the law to which he is subject, and who is of sound mind, may employ an agent.

Who may be an agent: As between the principal and third persons, any person may become an agent, but no person who is not of the age of majority and sound mind can become an agent, so as to be responsible to the principal according to the provisions in that behalf herein contained.

Consideration not necessary: No consideration is necessary to create an agency. Agent's authority may be express or implied: The authority of an agent may be express or implied.

Definitions of express and implied authority: An authority is said to be express when it is given by words spoken or written. An authority is said to be implied when it is to be inferred from the circumstances of the case; and things spoken or written, or the ordinary course of dealing, may be accounted circumstances of the case.

Illustration

Aman owns a shop in Serampur, living himself in Calcutta, and visiting the shop occasionally. Bharat manages the shop, and he is in the habit of ordering goods from Chaman in the name of Aman for the purposes of the shop, and of paying for them out of Aman's funds with Aman's knowledge. Bharat has an implied authority from Aman to order goods from Chaman in the name of Aman for the purpose of the shop. Extent of agent's authority:

An agent, having an authority to do an act, has authority to do every lawful thing, which is necessary in order to do such act. An agent having an authority to carry on a business has authority to do every lawful thing necessary for the purpose, or usually done in the course, of conducting such business.

Illustrations

(a) A is employed by B, residing in London, to recover at Bombay a debt due to B. A may adopt any legal process necessary for the purpose of recovering the debt, and may give a valid discharge for the same.

(b) A constitutes B his agent to carry on his business of a shipbuilder. B may purchase timber and other materials, and hire workmen, for the purpose of carrying on the business.

Agent's Authority in an Emergency: An agent has authority, in an emergency, to do all such acts for the purpose of protecting his principal from loss and would be done by a person or ordinary prudence, in his own case, under similar circumstances.

SUB AGENT

When Agent cannot Delegate

An agent cannot lawfully employ another to perform acts, which he has expressly, or impliedly undertaken to perform personally, unless by the ordinary custom of trade a sub-agent may, or, from the nature of agency, a sub-agent must, be employed.

"Sub-agent" Defined

A "sub-agent" is a person employed by, and acting under the control of, the original agent in the business of the agency.

Representation of Principal by Sub-agent Properly Appointed

Where a sub-agent is properly appointed, the principal is, so far as regards third persons, represented by the sub-agent, and is bound by and responsible for his acts, as if he were an agent originally appointed by the principal. Agent's responsibility for sub-agents: The agent is responsible to the principal for the acts of the sub-agent. Sub-agent's responsibility: The sub-agent is responsible for his acts to the agent, but not to the principal, except in case of fraud or willful wrong.

Agent's Responsibility for Sub-agent Appointed without Authority

Where an agent, without having authority to do so, has appointed a person to act as a sub-agent, the agent stands towards such person in the relation of a principal to an agent, and is responsible for his acts both to the principal and to third person; the principal is not represented, by or responsible for the acts of the person so employed, nor is that person responsible to the principal. Relation between principal and person duly appointed by agent to act in business of agency When an agent, holding an express or implied authority to name another person to act for the principal in the business of the agency, has named another person accordingly, such person is not a sub-agent, but an agent of the principal for such part of the business of the agency as is entrusted to him.

Agent's Duty in Naming such Person

In selecting such agent for his principal, an agent is bound to exercise the same amount of discretion as a man of ordinary prudence would exercise in his own case; and, if he does this, he is not responsible to the principal for the acts of negligence of the agent so selected.

Illustrations

A instructs B, a merchant, to buy a ship for him. B employs a ship-surveyor of good reputation to choose a ship for A. The surveyor makes the choice negligently and the ship turns out to be unseaworthy and is lost. B is not, but the surveyor is, responsible to A. Right of person as to acts done for him without his authority-effect of ratification

Where acts are done by one person on behalf of another, but without his knowledge or authority, he may elect to ratify or to disown such acts. If he ratifies them, the same effects will follow as if they had been performed by his authority. Ratification may be expressed or implied

Ratification may be expressed or may be implied in the conduct of the person on whose behalf the acts are done.

Illustrations

(a) A, without authority, buys goods, for B. Afterwards B sells them to C on his own account; B's conduct implies a ratification of the purchase made for him by A.

(b) A, without B's authority, lends B's money to C. Afterwards B accepts interest on the money from C. B's conduct implies a ratification of the loan. Knowledge requisite for valid ratification

No valid ratification can be made by a person whose knowledge of the facts of the case is materially defective.

Effect of ratifying unauthorized act forming part of a transaction

A person ratifying any unauthorized act done on his behalf ratifies the whole of the transaction of which such act formed a part.

Ratification of Unauthorized act cannot Injure Third Person

An act done by one person on behalf of another, without such other person's authority, which, if done with authority would have the effect of subjecting a third person to damages, or of terminating any right to interest of a third person cannot, by ratification, be made to have such effect.

REVOCATION OF AUTHORITY

Termination of Agency

An agency is terminated by the principal revoking his authority, or by the agent renouncing the business of the agency; or by the business of the agency being completed; or by either the principal or agent dying or becoming of unsound mind; or by the principal being adjudicated an insolvent under the provisions of any Act for the time being in force for the relief of insolvent debtors. Termination of agency, where agent has an interest in subject-matter Where the agent has himself an interest in the property, which forms the subject matter of the agency, the agency cannot, in the absence of an express contract, be terminated to the prejudice of such interest.

Illustration

A, gives authority to B to sell A's land, and to pay himself, out of the proceeds, the debts due to him from A.A cannot revoke this authority, nor can it be terminated by his insanity or death.

When principal may revoke agent's authority.

The principal may, save as is otherwise provided by the last preceding section, revoke the authority given to his agent at any time before the authority has been exercised, so as to bind the principal.

Revocation where authority has been partly exercised.

The principal cannot revoke the authority given to his agent after the authority has been partly exercised; so far as regards such acts and obligations as arise from acts already done in the agency. Compensation for revocation by principal, or renunciation by agent.

Where there is an express or implied contract that the agency should be continued for any period of time, the principal must make compensation to the agent, or the agent to the principal, as the case may be, for any previous revocation or renunciation of the agency without sufficient cause.

Notice of revocation or renunciation.

Reasonable notice must be given of such revocation or renunciation, otherwise the damage thereby resulting to the principal or the agent, as the case may be, must be made good to the one by the other.

Revocation and renunciation may be expressed or implied.

Revocation or renunciation may be expressed or may be implied in the conduct of that principal or agent respectively.

Illustration

A empowers B to let A's house. Afterwards A lets it himself. This is an implied revocation of B's authority.

When termination of agent's authority takes effect as to agent, and as to third persons.

The termination of the authority of an agent does not, so far as regards the agent, take effect before it becomes known to him, or, so far as regards third persons, before it becomes known to them.

Agent's duty on termination of agency by principal's death or insanity When an agency is terminated by the principal dying or becoming of unsound mind, the agent is bound to take on behalf of the representative, of his late principal, all reasonable steps for the protection and reservation of the interests entrusted to him.

Termination of Sub-agent's Authority

The termination of the authority of an agent causes the termination (subject to the rules herein contained regarding the termination of an agent's authority) of the authority of all sub-agents appointed by him.

AGENT'S DUTY TO PRINCIPAL

Agent's Duty in Conducting Principal's Business

An agent is bound to conduct the business of his principal according to the directions given by the principal, or in the absence of any such directions according to the customs, which prevails in doing business of the same kind at the place where the agent conducts such business. When the agent acts otherwise, if any loss be sustained, he must make it good to his principal and if any profit accrues, he must account for it.

Skill and Diligence required from Agent

An agent is bound to conduct the business of the agency with as much skill as is generally possessed by person engaged in similar business unless the principal has notice of his want of skill. The agent is always bound to act with reasonable diligence, and to use such skill as he possesses; and to make compensation to his principal in respect of the direct consequences of his own neglect, want of skill, or misconduct, but not in respect of loss or damage which are indirectly or remotely caused by such neglect, want of skill, or misconduct.

Agent's Accounts

An agent is bound to render proper accounts to his principal on demand. Agent's, duty to communicate with principal

It is the duty of an agent in case of difficulty, to use all reasonable diligence in communicating with his principal, and in seeking to obtain his instructions. Right of principal when agent deals, on his own account, in business of agency without principal's consent

If an agent deals on his own account in the business of the agency, without first obtaining the consent of his principal and acquainting him with all material circumstances, which have come to his own knowledge on the subject, the principal may .Repudiate the transaction, if the case shows, either that any material fact has been dishonestly concealed from him by the agent, or that the dealings of the agent have been disadvantageous to him.

Illustrations

(a) A direct B to sell A's estate. B buys the estate for himself in the name of C. A, on discovering that B has bought the estate for himself, may repudiate the sale, if he can show that B has dishonestly concealed any material fact, or that the seals has been disadvantageous to him.

(b) A directs B to sell A's estate. B, on looking over the estate before selling it, finds a mine on the estate which is unknown to A. B informs A that he wished to buy the estate for himself but conceals the discovery of the mine. A allows B to buy, in ignorance of the existence of the mine. A, on discovering that B knew of the mine at the time he bought the estate, may either repudiate or adopt the sale at his option.

Principal's right to benefit gained by agent dealing on his own account in business of agency.

If an agent, without the knowledge of his principal, deals in the business of the agency on his own account instead of on account to his principal, the principal is entitled to claim from the agent any benefit which may have resulted to him from the transaction.

Agent's right of retainer out of sums received on principal's account An agent may retain, out of any sums received on account of the principal in the business of the agency, all moneys due to himself in respect of advances made or expenses properly incurred by him in conducting such business, and also such remuneration as may be payable to him for acting as agent.

Agent's Duty to Pay sums received for Principal

Subject to such deductions, the agent is bound to pay to his principal all sums received on his account.

When agent's remuneration becomes due.

In the absence of any special contract, payment for the performance of any act is not due to the agent until the completion of such act; but an agent may detain moneys received by him on account of goods sold, although the whole of the goods consigned to him for sale may not have been sold, or although the sale may not be actually complete. Agent not entitled to remuneration for business misconduct.

An agent, who is guilty of misconduct in the business of the agency, is not entitled to any remuneration in respect of that part of the business, which he has misconducted.

Illustrations

A employs B to recover 1,000 rupees from C. Through B's misconduct the money is not recovered. B is entitled to no remuneration for his services and must make good the loss.

Agent's Lien on Principal's Property

In the absence of any contract to the contrary, an agent is entitled to retain goods, papers, and other property, whether movable or immovable of the principal received by him, until the amount due to himself for commission, disbursements and services in respect of the same has been paid or accounted for to him.

PRINCIPAL'S DUTY TO AGENT

Agent to be indemnified against consequences of lawful acts The employer of an agent is bound to indemnify him against the consequences of all lawful acts done by such agent in exercise of the authority conferred upon him. Agent to be indemnified against consequences of acts done in good faith Where one person employs another to do an act, and the agent does the act in good faith, the employer is liable to indemnify the agent against the consequences of that act, though it may cause an injury to the rights of third persons.

Non-liability of employer of agent to do a criminal act Where one person employees another to do an act which is criminal, the employer is not liable to the agent, either upon an express or an implied promise to indemnify him against the consequences of that Act.

Illustrations

A employs B to beat C, and agrees to indemnify him against all consequences of the act. B thereupon beats C, and has to pay damages to C for so doing. A is not liable to indemnify B for those damages. Compensation to agent for injury caused by principal's neglect. The principal must make compensation to his agent in respect of injury caused to such agent by the principal's neglect or want of skill.

Illustration

A employs B as a bricklayer in building a house, and put up the scaffolding himself. The scaffolding is unskillfully put up, and B is in consequence hurt. A must make compensation to B.

EFFECT OF AGENCY ON CONTRACTS WITH THIRD PERSONS

Enforcement and Consequences of Agent's Contract

Contracts entered into through an agent, and obligations arising from acts done by an agent, may be enforced in the same manner, and will have the same legal consequences as if the contracts had been entered into the acts done by the principal in person.

Illustrations

(a) A buys goods from B, knowing that he is an agent for their sale, but not knowing who the principal is. B's principal is the person entitled to claim from A the price of the goods, and A cannot, in a suit by the principal, set-off against that claim a debt due to himself from B.

(b) A, being B's agent; with authority to receive money on his behalf, receives from C a sum of money due to B. C is discharged of his obligation to pay the sum in question to B.

Principal how far Bound, when Agent exceeds Authority

When an agent does more than he is authorized to do, and when the part of what he does, which is within his authority, can be separated from the part, which is beyond his authority, so much only of what he does as is within his authority is binding as between him and his principal.

Principal not bound when excess of agent's authority is not separable Where an agent does more than he is authorized to do, and what he does beyond the scope of his authority cannot be separated from what is within it, the principal is not bound to recognize the transaction.

Illustration

A authorizes B to buy 500 sheep for him. B buys 500 sheep and 200 lambs for a sum of 6,000 rupees. A may repudiate the whole transaction.

Consequences of Notice given to Agent

Any notice given to or information obtained by the agent, provided it be given or obtained in the course of the business transacted by him for the principal, shall, as between the principal and third parties, have the same legal consequences as if it had been given to or obtained by the principal.

Illustrations

A is employed by B to buy from C goods of which C is the apparent owner. A was, before he was so employed a servant of C, and then learnt that the goods really belonged to D, but B is ignorant of that fact. In spite of the knowledge of his agent, B may set-off against the price of the goods a debt owing to him from C. Agent cannot personally enforce, nor be bound by, contracts on behalf of principal.

In the absence of any contract to that effect an agent cannot personally enforce contracts entered into by him on behalf of his principal, nor is he personally bound by them. Presumption of contract to the contrary: Such a contract shall be presumed to exit in the following cases-

(1) Where the contract is made by an agent for the sale or purchase of goods for a merchant resident abroad;

(2) Where agent does not disclose the name of his principal;

(3) Where the principal, though disclosed, cannot be sued.

Right of Parties to a Contract made by Agent not Disclosed

If an agent makes a contract with a person who neither, knows nor has reason to suspect, that he is an agent, his principal may require the performance of the contract; but the other contracting party has, as against the principal, the same right as he would have had as against if the agent had been the principal.

If the principal discloses himself before the contract is completed, the other contracting party may refuse to fulfill the contract, if he can show that, if he had known who was the principal in the contract, or if he had known that the agent was not a principal, he would not have entered into the contract.

Performance of Contract with Agent Supposed to be Principal

Where one man makes a contract with another, neither knowing nor having reasonable ground to suspect that the other is an agent, the principal, if he requires the performance of the contract, can only obtain such performance subject to the right and obligations subsisting between the agent and the other party of the contract. Liability of principal inducing belief that agent's unauthorized acts were authorized.

When an agent has, without authority, done acts or incurred obligations to third person on behalf of his principal, the principal is bound by such acts or obligations, if he has by his word or conduct induced such third person to believe that such acts and obligations were within the scope of the agent's authority.

Illustrations

(a) A consigns goods to B for sale, and gives him instructions not to sell under a fixed price. C, being ignorant of B's instruction, enters into a contract with B to buy the goods at a price lower than the reserved price. A is bound by the contract

(b) A entrusts B with negotiable instruments endorsed in blank. B sells them to C in violation of private order from A. The sale is good.

Effect, on agreement, of misrepresentation or fraud by agent.

Misrepresentation made or fraud committed, by agent acting in the course of their business for their principals, have the same effect on agreements made by such agents as if such misrepresentations of frauds had been made or committed by the principals; but misrepresentations made, or frauds committed, by agents, in matters which do not affect their authority, do not affect their principals

Illustrations

(a) A, being B's agent for the sale of goods, induces C to buy them by a misrepresentation, which he was not authorized by B to make. The contract is voidable, as between B and C, at the option of C.

(c) A, the captain of B's ship, signs bills of lading without having received on board the goods mentioned therein. The bills of lading are void as between B and the pretended consignor.

CONSUMER PROTECTION ACT, 1986

The Consumer Protection Act was passed by the Parliament in 1986 and it came into force from 1987. Its purposes to protect consumers against defective goods, unsatisfactory services, unfair trade practices, etc. The Act provides for three-tier machinery consisting of District Forum, State Commission and National Commission. It also provides for the formation protection councils in every state. The consumers can file their complaints at the appropriate forum for quick redressal. The complaint may relate to defective refrigerator or TV set, nonfunctional telephone, lack of due cares in medical treatment and so on. Any service or product given free of charge is not covered by the Act.

Definitions of Important Terms

Before studying the provisions of the CPA, it is necessary to understand the terms used in the Act. Let us understand some of the more important definitions. Complainant means:-

1. A consumer; or
2. Any voluntary consumer association registered under the Companies Act, 1956 or under any other law for the time being in force; or

3. The Central Government or any State Government, who or which makes a complaint; or
4. One or more consumers where there are numerous consumers having the same interest

Complaint means any allegation in writing made by a complainant that:-

1. an unfair trade practice or a restricted trade practice has been adopted by any trader
2. the goods bought by him or agreed to be bought by him suffer from one more defects
3. the services hired or availed of or agreed to be hired or availed of by him suffer from deficiency in any respect
4. the trader has charged for the goods mentioned in the complaint a price excess of the price fixed by or under any law for the time being in force or displayed on the goods or any package containing such goods.
5. goods which will be hazardous to life and safety when used, are being offered for sale to the public in contravention of the provisions of any law for the time being in force, requiring traders to display information in regard to the contents, manner and effect of use of such goods; with a view to obtaining any relief provided by law under the CPA.

Consumer means any person who:-

1. buys any goods for a consideration which has been paid or promised or partly paid and partly promised, or under any system of deferred payment (for example hire purchase or installment sales) and includes any other user of such goods when such use is made with the approval of the buyer, but does not include a person who obtains such goods for resale or for any commercial purpose; or
2. hires or avails of any services for a consideration which has been paid or promised, or partly paid and partly

promised, or under any system of deferred payment and includes any beneficiary of such services when such services are availed of with the approval of the first mentioned person For the purposes of this definition "commercial purpose" does not include use by a consumer of goods bought and used by him exclusively for the purpose of earning his livelihood by means of self-employment.

Goods mean goods as defined in the Sale of Goods Act, 1930. Under that act, goods means every kind of movable property other than actionable claims and money and includes stocks and shares, growing crops, grass and things attached to or forming part of the land which are agreed to be severed before sale or under the contract of sale. Service is defined to mean service of any description which is made available to potential users and includes the provision of facilities in connection with banking, financing, insurance, transport, processing, supply of electrical or other energy, board or lodging or both, housing construction, entertainment, amusement or the purveying of news or other information but does not include the rendering of any service free of charge or under a contract of personal service.

Consumer dispute means dispute where the person against whom a complaint has been made, denies or disputes the allegation contained in the complaint. Restrictive Trade Practice means any trade practice which requires a consumer to buy, hire, or avail of any good or as the case may be, services as a condition precedent for buying, hiring or availing of any other goods or services.

Unfair Trade Practice means unfair trade practice as defined under the Monopolies and Restrictive Trade Practices Act. The MRPT act has defined certain practices to be unfair trade practices.

Defect means any fault, imperfection or shortcoming in the quality, quantity, potency, purity or standard which is required to be maintained by or under any law for the time being in force or under any contract, express or implied, or as is claimed by the trade in any manner whatsoever in relation to any goods.

Deficiency means any fault, imperfection or shortcoming or inadequacy in the quality, nature and manner of performance which is required to be maintained by or under any law for the time being in force or has been undertaken to be performed by a person in pursuance of a contract or otherwise in relation to any service. A consumer is a user of goods and services. Any person paying for goods and services, which he uses, is entitled to expect that the goods and services be of a nature and quality promised to him by the seller.

The earlier principle of "Caveat Emptor" or "let the buyer beware" which was prevalent has given way to the principle of "Consumer is King". The origins of this principle lie in the fact that in today's mass production economy where there is little contact between the producer and consumer, often sellers make exaggerated claims and advertisements, which they do not intend to fulfill. This leaves the consumer in a difficult position with very few avenues for redressal. The onset on intense competition also made producers aware of the benefits of customer satisfaction and hence by and large, the principle of "consumer is king" is now accepted.

Objects of the Consumer Protection Act, 1986

The preamble to the Act states that the Act is legislated to provide for better protection of the interests of consumers and for that purpose to make provision for the establishment of consumer councils and other authorities for the settlement of consumer's disputes and for matters connected therewith. The CPA extends to the whole of India except the State of Jammu and Kashmir and applies to all goods and services unless otherwise notified by the Central Government. The basic rights of consumers as per the Consumer Protection Act (CPA) are:

1. Right to safety.
2. Right to be informed.

3. Right to choose.
4. Right to representation (or to be heard).
5. Right to seek redressal.
6. Right to consumer education.

1. *Right to Safety* It is the consumer right to be protected against goods and services which is hazardous to health or life.
2. *Right to be Informed* The consumer has the right to be informed about the quality, quantity, purity, standard and price of goods he intends to purchase. Therefore, the manufacture must mention complete information about the product, its ingredients, date of manufacture, price, precaution of use, etc. on the label and package of the product.
3. *Right to Choose* The consumer should be assured of freedom to choose from a variety of products at competitive prices. Every consumer wants to buy a product on his free will. There should be free competition in the market so that the consumer may make the right choice in satisfying his needs.
4. *Right to Representation (or to be Heard)* The consumer has a right to register dissatisfaction with any product and get his complaint heard. Most of the reputed firms have set up consumer service cells to listen to the consumer's complaint and take appropriate steps to redress their grievances.
5. *Right to Seek Redressal.* It is the right to seek redressal against any defect in goods or unfair trade suffered by the consumer. If the quality and performance of a product falls short of seller's claims, the consumer has a right to certain remedies. The Consumer Protection Act requires that the product must be repaired, replaced or taken back by the seller as provided under the contract between the buyer and the seller.

6. *Right to Consumer Education.* It means right of acquiring knowledge and being a well-informed consumer throughout his life. He should also be made aware of his rights and the remedies available through publicity in the mass media.

Consumer Responsibilities

(i) *To provide adequate information to the seller* The consumer has the responsibility to provide adequate information about his needs and expectation to the sellers.

(ii) *To exercise caution in purchasing* The consumer must try to get full information on the quality, design, utility, quantity, price, etc. of the product before purchasing it.

(iii) *To insist on cash memo or receipt* The consumer must get a cash memo or receipt as a proof of purchase of goods from the seller. This would help him in making a complaint to the seller in case of any defect in the goods.

(iv) *To file complaint against genuine grievance* The consumer must file a complaint with the seller or manufacturer about any defects or shortcoming in the products and services.

(v) *To be quality conscious* The consumer should never compromise on the quality of goods. While making purchases, the consumers must look for standard quality certification marks such as ISI, Agmark, Woolmark, FPO, etc. For example, electric iron must carry ISI mark.

Redressal Machinery under the Act

Consumer Protection Councils

The interests of consumers are enforced through various authorities set up under the CPA. The CPA provides for the setting up of the Central Consumer Protection Council, the State Consumer Protection Council and the District Forum.

Central Consumer Protection Council

The Central Government has set up the Central Consumer Protection Council, which consists of the following members:-

(a) The Minister in charge of Consumer Affairs in the Central Government who is its Chairman, and

(b) Other official and non-official members representing varied interests

The Central council consists of 150 members and its term is 3 years. The Council meets as and when necessary but at least one meeting is held in a year.

State Consumer Protection Council

The State Council consists of:-

(a) The Minister in charge of Consumer Affairs in the State Government who is its Chairman, and

(b) Other official and non-official members representing varied interests The State Council meets as and when necessary but not less than two meetings must be held every year.

Redressal Machinery under the Act

The CPA provides for a 3-tier approach in resolving consumer disputes.

The District Forum has jurisdiction to entertain complaints where the value of goods / services complained against and the compensation claimed is less than Rs. 20 lakhs, the State Commission for claims exceeding Rs. 20 lakhs but not exceeding Rs. 1crore and the National Commission for claims exceeding Rs.1 crore.

District Forum

Under the CPA, the State Government has to set up a district Forum in each district of the State. The government may establish more than one District Forum in a district if it deems fit. Each District Forum consists of:-

(a) A person who is, or who has been, or is qualified to be, a District Judge who shall be its President

(b) Two other members who shall be persons of ability, integrity and standing and have adequate knowledge or experience of or have shown capacity in dealing with problems relating to economics, law, commerce, accountancy, industry, public affairs or administration, one of whom shall be a woman.

Appointments to the State Commission shall be made by the State Government on the recommendation of a Selection Committee consisting of the President of the State Committee, the Secretary-Law Department of the State and the secretary in charge of Consumer Affairs Every member of the District Forum holds office for 5 years or up to the age of 65 years, whichever is earlier and is not eligible for re-appointment. A member may resign by giving notice in writing to the State Government whereupon the vacancy will be filled up by the State Government.

The District Forum can entertain complaints where the value of goods or services and the compensation, if any, claimed is less than rupees twenty lakhs. However, in addition to jurisdiction over consumer goods services valued upto Rs.20 lakhs, the District Forum also may pass orders against traders indulging in unfair trade practices, sale of defective goods or render deficient services provided the turnover of goods or value of services does not exceed rupees twenty lakhs. A complaint shall be instituted in the District Forum within the local limits of whose jurisdiction-

(a) The opposite party or the defendant actually and voluntarily resides or carries on business or has a branch office or personally works for gain at the time of institution of the complaint; or

(b) Any one of the opposite parties (where there are more than one) actually and voluntarily resides or carries on business or has a branch office or personally works for gain, at the time of institution of the complaint provided that the other opposite party/parties acquiescence in such institution or the permission of the Forum is obtained in respect of such opposite parties; or

(c) The cause of action arises, wholly or in part.

State Commission

The Act provides for the establishment of the State Consumer Disputes Redressal Commission by the State Government in the State by notification. Each State Commission shall consist of:-

(a) A person who is or has been a judge of a High Court appointed by State Government (in consultation with the Chief Justice of the High Court) who shall be its President;

(b) Two other members who shall be persons of ability, integrity, and standing and have adequate knowledge or experience of, or have shown capacity in dealing with, problems relating to economics, law, commerce, accountancy, industry, public affairs or administration, one of whom must be a woman.

Every appointment made under this is made by the State Government on the recommendation of a Selection Committee consisting of the President of the State Commission, Secretary-Law Department of the State and Secretary in charge of Consumer Affairs in the State.

Every member of the District Forum holds office for 5 years or upto the age of 65 years, whichever is earlier and is not eligible for re-appointment. A member may resign by giving notice in writing to the State Government whereupon the vacancy will be filled up by the State Government.

The State Commission can entertain complaints where the value of goods or services and the compensation, if any, exceeds Rs. 20 lakhs but does not exceed Rs. 1crore.

The State Commission also has the jurisdiction to entertain appeal against the orders of any District Forum within the

State The State Commission also has the power to call for the records and appropriate orders in any consumer dispute which is pending before or has been decided by any District Forum within the State if it appears that such District Forum has exercised any power not vested in it by law or has failed to exercise a power rightfully vested in it by law or has acted illegally or with material irregularity.

National Commission

The Central Government provides for the establishment of the National Consumer Disputes Redressal Commission The National Commission shall consist of:-

(a) A person who is or has been a judge of the Supreme Court, to be appoint by the Central Government (in consultation with the Chief Justice of India) who be its President;

(b) Four other members who shall be persons of ability, integrity and standing and have adequate knowledge or experience of, or have shown capacity in dealing with, problems relating to economics, law, commerce, accountancy, industry, public affairs or administration, one of whom shall be a woman

Appointments shall be by the Central Government on the recommendation of a Selection Committee consisting of a Judge of the Supreme Court to be nominated by the Chief Justice of India, the Secretary in the Department of Legal Affairs and the Secretary in charge of Consumer Affairs in the Government of India. Every member of the National Commission shall hold office for a term of five years or upto seventy years of age, whichever is earlier and shall not be eligible for reappointment. The National Commission shall have jurisdiction:-

a. to entertain complaints where the value of the goods or services and the compensation, if any, claimed exceeds rupees one crores:

b. to entertain appeals against the orders of any State Commission; and

c. to call for the records and pass appropriate orders in any consumer dispute which is pending before, or has been decided by any State Commission where it appears to the National Commission that such Commission has exercised a jurisdiction not vested in it by law, or has failed to exercise a jurisdiction so vested, or has acted in the exercise of its jurisdiction illegally or with material irregularity.

Complaints may be filed with the District Forum by:-

1. The consumer to whom such goods are sold or delivered or agreed to be sold or delivered or such service provided or agreed to be provided
2. Any recognized consumer association, whether the consumer to whom goods sold or delivered or agreed to be sold or delivered or service provided or agreed to be provided, is a member of such association or not
3. One or more consumers, where there are numerous consumers having the same interest with the permission of the District Forum, on behalf of or for the benefit of, all consumers so interested
4. The Central or the State Government.

On receipt of a complaint, a copy of the complaint is to be referred to the opposite party, directing him to give his version of the case within 30 days. This period may be extended by another 15 days. If the opposite party admits the allegations contained in the complaint, the complaint will be decided on the basis of materials on the record. Where the opposite party denies or disputes the allegations or omits or fails to take any action to represent his case within the time provided, the dispute will be settled in the following manner:-

In case of dispute relating to any goods: Where the complaint alleges a defect in the goods which cannot be determined without proper analysis or test of the goods, a sample of the goods shall be obtained from the complainant, sealed and authenticated in the manner prescribed for referring to the appropriate laboratory for the purpose of any analysis or test whichever may be necessary, so as to find out whether such goods suffer from any other defect.

The appropriate laboratory' would be required to report its finding to the referring authority, i.e. the District Forum or the State Commission within a period of forty-five days from the receipt of the reference or within such extended period as may be granted by these agencies.

Limitation Period for Filing of Complaint

The District Forum, the State Commission, or the National Commission shall not admit a complaint unless it is filed within two years from the date on which the cause of action has arisen. However, where the complainant satisfies the District Forum / State Commission, that he had sufficient cause for not filing the complaint within two years, such complaint may be entertained by it after recording the reasons for condoning the delay.

Powers of the Redressal Agencies

The District Forum, State Commission and the National Commission are vested with the powers of a civil court under the Code of Civil Procedure while trying a suit in respect of the following matters:-

1. The summoning and enforcing attendance of any defendant or witness examining the witness on oath;
2. The discovery and production of any document or other material producible as evidence;
3. The reception of evidence on affidavits:
4. The requisitioning of the report of the concerned analysis or test from the appropriate laboratory or from any other relevant source;
5. Issuing of any commission for the examination of any witness; and
6. Any other matter which may be prescribed.

Under the Consumer Protection Rules, 1987, the District Forum, Commission and the National Commission have the power to require any person:-

(i) To produce before, and allow to be examined by an officer of any authorities, such books of accounts, documents or commodities as may be required and to keep such book, documents etc. under its custody for the purposes of the Act;

(ii) To furnish such information which may be required for the purposes to any officer so specified.

They have the power to:-

(i) To pass written orders authorizing any officer to exercise power of entry and search of any premises where these books, papers, commodities, or documents are kept if there is any ground to believe that these may be destroyed, altered, falsified or secreted. Such authorized officer may also seize books, papers, documents or commodities if they are required for the purposes of the Act, provided the seizure is communicated to the District Forum / State Commission / National commission within 72 hours.

On examination of such documents or commodities, the agency concerned may order the retention thereof or may return it to the party concerned.

(ii) to issue remedial orders to the opposite party.

(iii) to dismiss frivolous and vexatious complaints and to order the complainant to make payment of costs, not exceeding Rs. 10,000 to the opposite party.

Remedies Granted under the Act

The District Forum / State Commission / National Commission may pass one or more of the following orders to grant relief to the aggrieved consumer:-

1. To remove the defects pointed out by the appropriate laboratory from goods in question;
2. To replace the goods with new goods of similar description, which shall be free from any defect;

3. To return to the complainant the price, or, as the case may be, the charges paid by the complainant;
4. To pay such amount as may be awarded by it as compensation to the consumer for any loss or injury suffered by the consumer due to negligence of the opposite party;
5. To remove the defects or deficiencies in the services in question;
6. To discontinue the unfair trade practice or the restrictive trade practice or not to repeat them;
7. Not to offer the hazardous goods for sale:
8. To withdraw the hazardous goods from being offered for sale:
9. To provide for adequate costs to parties.

Appeals

Any person aggrieved by an order made by the Forum may prefer an appeal to the State Commission in the prescribed form and manner.

Similarly, any person aggrieved by any original order of the State Commission may prefer an appeal to the National Commission in the prescribed form and manner. Any person aggrieved by any original order of the National Commission may prefer an appeal to the Supreme Court.

All such appeals are to be made within thirty days from the date of the order provided that the concerned Appellate authority may entertain an appeal after the said period of thirty days if it is satisfied that there was sufficient cause for not filling it within that period.

The period of 30 days is to be computed from the date of receipt of the order by the appellant. Where no appeal has been preferred against any of the orders of the authorities, such orders would be final. The District Forum, State Commission or National Commission may enforce respective orders as if it was a decree or order made by a Court and in the event of their inability to execute the same; they may send the order to the Court for execution by it as if it were a Court decree or order.

Penalties

Failure or omission by a trader or other person against whom a complaint is made or the complainant to comply with any order of the State Commission or the National Commission shall be punishable with imprisonment for a term which shall not be less than one month but which may extend to 3 years, or with fine of not less than Rs. 2,000 but which may to Rs. 10000 or with both.

However, if it is satisfied that the circumstances of any case so requires, then the District Forum or the State Commission or the National Commission may impose a lower fine or a shorter term of imprisonment.

SUMMARY

During the mushrooming of insurance companies many financially unsound concerns were also floated which failed miserably.

The Insurance Act 1938 was the first legislation governing not only life insurance but also non-life insurance to provide strict state control over insurance business. The demand for nationalization of life insurance industry was made repeatedly in the past but it gathered momentum in 1944 when a bill to amend the Life Insurance Act 1938 was introduced in the Legislative Assembly.

However, it was much later on the 19th of January, 1956, that life insurance in India was nationalized. About 154 Indian insurance companies, 16 non-Indian companies and 75 provident were operating in India at the time of nationalization.

Nationalization was accomplished in two stages; initially the management of the companies was taken over by means of an Ordinance, and later, the ownership too by means of a comprehensive bill.

The Parliament of India passed the Life Insurance Corporation Act on the 19th of June 1956, and the Life Insurance Corporation of India was created on 1st September, 1956, with the objective of spreading life insurance much more widely and in particular to the rural areas with a view to reach all insurable persons in the country, providing them adequate financial cover at a reasonable cost.

The IRDA Bill provides for the establishment of an authority to protect the interests of the holders of insurance policies, to regulate, promote and insure orderly growth of the insurance industry and amend the Insurance Act, 1938, the Life Insurance Act, 1956 and the General Insurance Business (Nationalization) Act, 1972.

The bill allows foreign equity stake in domestic private insurance companies to a maximum of 26 per cent of the total paid-up capital and seeks to provide statutory status to the insurance regulator. The insurance business in India is pegged at $ 6.6 Billion whereas industry leaders feel privatization will increase it to $ 40 Billion within next 3-5 years.

5

FURURE PROSPECTS OF INSURANCE

INTRODUCTION

In addition to life, fire and marine Insurance, several other general types of insurances are available today. The nationalized general insurance companies have also been offering special schemes meant for rural areas such as crop insurance, cattle insurance, insurance for huts, poultry etc. There is also a social security group accident scheme covering weaker sections of the society. Some of these are described below:

Personal Accident Insurance

All of us are exposed to the risk of accident, which is a threat to our financial security, and therefore it is prudent to have adequate personal accident cover to manage this contingency. For handling accident risks, personal accident policy, Janata personal accident policy and Gramin personal accident policies are available in India.

Scope of Cover

Personal accident policy pays compensation to the insured in the event of happening of one or more of the following listed below which may be selected by insured at the time of taking policy:

- On death
- On permanent total and partial disability and
- On temporary total disability

In case of accident death during the policy period, the policy in addition covers funeral expenses of the insured person. Permanent total disablement occurs when an individual is unable to perform his regular duties for the remaining part of his life. Permanent partial disablement may result when a person loses any part of his body due to accident.

When an individual is injured in an accident and as a result he is unable to perform his normal duties for a certain period we can describe it as temporary total disablement. This policy can also be extended to reimburse the medical expenses due to accidents up to 10% of the insured amount or 25% of the claim amount or expenses incurred for treatment of the insured person whichever is less. Personal accident policy does not cover the injuries resulting out of war, self-inflicted injury, diseases or insanity, death due to war operations, attempted suicides, accident in armed forces, aircraft accidents, accidents due to nuclear weapons etc.

Janata personal accident policy is meant for weaker section of the society. Thus premium charged under this policy is comparatively less. Gramin personal accident policy is designed for the rural people in the country. It is a contract of Insurance under which the insurer agrees to pay a specific sum of money to the insured in case of bodily injury by accident and to the heirs of the insured in case of death by accident. A contract of personal accident insurance is not a contract of indemnity and the insurer has to pay a fixed sum of money on the death or total disablement of the insured or provide medical benefits for recovery from the injury.

In case of accidental death during the policy period, the policy in addition covers funeral expenses of the insured person. Permanent total disablement occurs when an individual is unable to perform his regular duties for the remaining part of his life. Permanent partial disablement may result when a person loses any part of his body due to accident. It does not cover the injuries resulting out of war, diseases, attempted suicides etc.

Fidelity Insurance

Under this type of insurance contract the insurer undertakes to compensate the insured against the loss caused by misappropriation of funds or goods or damage to the property caused by his employees.

Such a policy is useful to the employers who fear embezzlement, forgery, fraud and dishonesty on the part of their employees. Under it the insured is required to furnish all material facts about the employees and also to notify any change in the condition of their service. The policy can be taken for specific positions rather than names, e.g., accountant, cashier etc. Blanket cover is also available for entire staff or group of employees.

Burglary Insurance

Such a policy provides protection against loss or damage caused by housebreaking, robbery or theft. It is also known as 'robbery, theft or larceny insurance'. For this purpose a comprehensive policy may be taken or each risk may be separately insured. Full details of the article insured are given in the policy. Insured items include gold and gold ornaments and other assets including household items such as TV, fridge, air conditioner etc. A burglary policy for business premises would provide cover against loss to damage by house breaking and burglary of stock-in-trade, goodsin-transit, cash-in-safe, fixture and fittings etc.

Credit Insurance

Credit insurance policy is taken to cover the loss which may arise due to bad debts or non-payment of dues by the debtors. This insurance is very useful to businessmen who sell goods on credit. It protects them from loss arising out of insolvency of their debtors. In India, Export Credit and Guarantee Corporation (ECGC) provides credit insurance to exporters.

Workmen's Compensation Insurance

In India, Workmen's Compensation Act was passed in 1934 and 1946. According to this act, an employer is required to pay compensation to his workers who receive injuries or contract occupational diseases during the course of their work. An employer may obtain an insurance policy to cover such liability. The premiums are payable usually on the basis of wages. It is also known as 'Employers Liability Insurance'. This policy is essential to every employer who employs 'workmen' as defined under the Workmen's Compensation Act in order to protect himself against the legal liabilities arising out of death or bodily injury to this workman. It also extends coverage through reimbursement of medical, surgical and hospitalization expenses including transportation costs on the payment of additional premium. The National Insurance Company Ltd, United India Insurance Company Ltd, Oriental Insurance Company Ltd, and the New India Assurance Company Ltd offer workmen's compensation policies.

Travel Insurance

Travel insurance covers travel related accidents also. While traveling outside India, individuals face risks such as loss of baggage, accidents involving injuries, illnesses and medical emergencies requiring hospitalization treatment. All this can pose serious consequences to the overseas travellers. A rational person should therefore secure the required coverage before leaving his home country. In India travel insurance has become popular among International travellers. The coverage offered under travel insurance policies in India are as follows

Wedding Insurance

These days, weddings have become quite an expensive and elaborate affair. People do take care to make this once-in-a-lifetime event a memorable one. In case of any postponement or cancellation, there is a certain risk of monetary loss. The wedding insurance package can compensate for the monetary loss. This unique product covers the specific risks related to weddings. This Policy can protect you against certain types of financial losses you may incur in the event of unpredictable situations during the period leading up to and including your wedding day.

The period of insurance will be 24 hours prior to the start of the customary functions or rituals or programmes of events mentioned in the printed invitations till the end of the function or five days from the beginning whichever occurs earlier.

This policy provides cover for expenses actually and already incurred or advances paid in connection with marriage hall, catering, pandit, guests, music parties, photos and videography, loss on cancellation of travel tickets etc. Liability is restricted only when such cancellation arises out of cancellation or postponement of marriage.

The policy does not cover any loss arises when marriage is cancelled or postponed because of dispute between marriage parties, willful negligence and criminal misconduct of the bride, bridegroom or their parents.

Employee State Insurance Scheme

The Employee State Insurance Scheme (ESIS) is an insurance system which provides both the cash and medical benefits. It is managed by the Employee State Insurance Corporation (ESIC), a wholly government-owned enterprise. It was conceived as a compulsory social security benefit for workers in the formal sector. The original legislation creating the scheme allowed it to cover only factories which has been using power and employing 10 or more workers. However, since 1989 the scheme has been expanded, and it now includes all such factories which are not using power and employing 20 or more persons. Mines and plantations are explicitly excluded from coverage under the ESIS Act.

Unemployment Insurance

Unemployment insurance is designed to provide short term protection for regularly employed persons who lose their jobs and who are willing and able to work. Unemployment insurance has several basic objectives:

1) Provide cash income during involuntary unemployment.
2) Help unemployed workers find jobs.
3) Encourage employees to stabilize employment.
4) Help stabilize economy.

Unemployment insurance is a popular concept in developed countries like U.S. where they have well defined laws and regulations. However in India it will take a long time to come.

Personal Liability Insurance

Personal liability insurance provides protection against the legal liability, which arises due to insured's personal acts. The insurance company will pay for legal defense to third party damages or injuries up to policy limit. Except legal liability, which arises due to automobile accidents and professional liability, most other personal acts are covered under personal liability insurance. The personal liability insurance covers damages caused to properties and injuries to other people due to the negligence of the insured. Under this policy, the insurance company is bound to defend the insured, should the matter go to court of law. It can also settle the matter out of court by negotiating with parties for a settlement within the policy limit. Personal liability policy offers very wide coverage. The following instances of loss, damages or injuries caused by an insured individual come under the purview of personal liability insurance in which coverage will be available up to the policy limit.

- Accidental fire to neighbors house as a result of insured's negligence
- Accidental injury to a third party while playing
- Damaging costly antique accidentally belonging to neighbor
- Injuring another person while riding a bicycle

Summary

We have seen that the entire non-life business has been divided into three segments, namely, Fire, Marine and

Miscellaneous insurance. Motor and Health are part of Miscellaneous insurance.

Fire insurance is the protection against a loss suffered by the insured as a result of damage caused by fire to the property covered by the policy. Like any other insurance contract it has to satisfy the essentials of a valid contract. e.g. indemnity, insurable interest, utmost good faith etc. Then we have seen the meaning of fire, different types of fire policies and claim settlement procedure.

In marine insurance, the insurer undertakes to indemnify the insured against the losses incidental to marine adventure. Then we have seen characteristics of general insurance, common to marine insurance. The meaning of marine perils, different marine insurance policies, types of marine insurance and types of losses, Clauses and Warranties are also explained. We have tried to understand how the concept of marine insurance evolves specially in India. Health insurance is a safeguard against rising medical costs. Different types of health insurance policies have been explained.

In India, motor insurance is classified as miscellaneous. It comes under tariff category and it offers policies and coverage at standard premium rate. We have also covered the basic principles of motor insurance, classification of vehicles, risks under motor insurance and claim settlement procedure. Miscellaneous insurance is a large portfolio and has numerous types of policies floated by different insurance companies. For the purpose of this lesson, miscellaneous insurance has been explained through Personal accident insurance, Fidelity insurance, Burglary insurance, Credit insurance, Travel insurance, Workmen's Compensation insurance, Wedding insurance, Employee State Insurance Scheme, Unemployment Insurance and Personal liability Insurance.

BOOMING SECTOR

The reforms in the insurance sector leading finally to the opening of the insurance sector for private participation have brought in its wake major changes not only in the design of the products available in the market but also the manner in which they are marketed. We have today a host of products coupled with a large number of intermediaries who market them.

The post-liberalized insurance industry panorama in India is witnessing dramatic changes in terms of a slew of latest products and services, new channels of distribution, greater use of I.T. as a service facilitator etc. There is also the phenomenon of noticeable shifts in consumer preferences impacting the product mix being offered by insurers. The market structure dominated by a few stabilized public sector players and the 'new' players in the market (some of whom claim their lineage from established international insurance behemoths) is in a state of flux-in terms of figure out market shares but is full of potential.

Added to these are the rising trends of convergence of financial services, especially in the areas like wealth management and evolution of newer risk management tools, particularly in the context of reinsurance management. Greater attention is also being bestowed on the areas like Agricultural Insurance and risk coverage of export-import trade. Then there is impact of visible socio-economic changes like greater urbanization, greater job mobility, growth of the services industry, weakening of traditional family structure, impact of globalization etc. All in all, interesting things are happening in the Indian insurance scene.

*Insurance undergone rapid and massive changes in all aspects of their business: product and services, sectoral structure, market segmentation, competitive environment.*It is believed that the information sharing has not taken its expected shape in the insurance industry for the purposes of practices, research and education. However, data is one of the most needed ingredients in the insurance business development as well as for research and consultancy. There have been regular efforts by IRDA for collection and sharing of the data and other information of public interest. The industry is facing problems in terms of data review as parliament need to register this beforehand. We believe that progress of the industry should not be constrained by any extraneous conditions in the interest of research and development in the area.

Manpower India today released the Manpower Employment Outlook Survey for the first quarter of 2006 revealing sustained positive hiring intentions of employers in India. India continues to lead all 23 countries surveyed this quarter, with a positive overall Net Employment Outlook of +27%. Even though this figure represents a decrease of 13 percentage points from the fourth quarter of 2005, the employment outlook remains extremely healthy. *For the first time since the Survey was launched in India, the Finance, Insurance and Retail industry sector emerged as the most optimistic sector for a quarter with a Net Employment Outlook of +32%, surpassing the Services sector.*

Privatization of insurance sector has allowed insurance companies to work in the market by depositing 100 crore rupees in the reserve of government. This has encouraged many overseas insurance companies, having a required amount in their reserve, to open their branch in our country. Introduction of the sector has changed the employment pattern, but people must know how to make profit from it. To be in the global market and have advantage of it, capital and skill as per the demand and knowledge of market is the requirement. It is necessary that institutions, which form a part of this financial system, have internal management, governance and accountability structures, which measure up to the highest standards.

CLASSIFICATION AND REVIEW OF RISK

Once all of the information is available, underwriter from insurance company evaluates the data. At this evaluation, the underwriter wants to classify the risk attached to the proposal. If the risk is more than what the insurance company is willing to bear for that proposal, the application is rejected by the underwriter. If the risk attached to the proposal is within the limits acceptable to the company, the proposal is accepted.

Then the underwriter decides the category in which the risk falls and premium to be paid is calculated accordingly. In the underwriting process, the life insurance agent gives the details of information required by the underwriter.

ENTERING THE PROPOSAL IN PROPOSAL REGISTER

When the proposal is consistent with the rules and the company decides to accept the proposal it is serially numbered and entered in the Proposal Register and Review Slip is made. For every proposal a different file is made containing review slip and other particulars related to the proposal.

SENDING ACCEPTANCE LETTER

The acceptance letter is sent by the insurance company to the proposer. The reminder of the payment of the premium due is also sent to the insured from time to time by the insurance company.

ISSUE OF FIRST PREMIUM RECEIPT

After the acceptance of proposal and payment of premium by the proposer, the insurance company will send First Premium Receipt to the proposer.

POLICY WRITING

The policy is usually written in a special department whose main task is to issue written contracts in accordance with the instructions from the underwriting department.

They also keep a register of policies for future reference. These days, insurance companies are using computers to keep records of clients, the payment of premium and other particulars.

SERVICING OF POLICY-HOLDERS

Servicing of policy holders include:

(1) Proof of age

(2) Nomination

(3) Assignment

(4) Alteration / Changes

(5) Paid up value & surrender value

PROOF OF AGE

The age of the life assured must be proved either during the period of the policy or after the claim arises, because age is an important factor for calculating at the rate of premium to be charged for a particular policy. The age is generally admitted by the following proofs.

(i) Certified extract from Municipal or other records made at the time of birth.

(ii) Original horoscope prepared at the time of birth. If it is found that the horoscope has been prepared for the specific purpose of proving the assured's age, the same should not be accepted.

(iii) Certificate of school or college records if the age or date of birth is stated therein.

(iv) Certificated extracts from the Service Registers of the reputed employer.

(v) Indemnity Cards issued by the Defence Department for its employees.

(vi) Passport issued by Passport Authority of India

(vii) Marriage certificate in case of Roman Catholics issued by Roman Catholic Church.

Cases where admission of age proof is required necessarily at the time of issue of policy.

The age should be proved at the time of issue of policy where the age of the life assured is below 20 or 50 and above, Children's Deferred Assurance Policies, Annuity Policies and policies issued under Salary Saving Scheme. Proof of age is an important issue for insurer as the older people have higher probability of death than the younger ones. So premium rates are calculated on the basis of age groups. Where the insured is unable to give any of the standard age proofs, the insured may accept the age on the basis of a 'Declaration of age' executed by an elderly relative or friend who has personal knowledge of the assured's date of birth. The declaration is required to be adequately stamped according to the stamp regulations. It must be signed by the declarant in the presence of a Magistrate or an officer empowered to administer oaths.

On submission of an age proof, age admission certificate is issued to the policyholder. In case of any difference in recorded age and actual age, the proposal review slip and policy register sheet are corrected accordingly. In case the actual age proves to be lower the excess of premiums charged from the policyholder will be refunded to him.

ASSIGNMENT AND NOMINATION

The Policyholder should be advised for nomination, if no nomination was effected. When nomination or assignment is effected by a policyholder, it should be scrutinized thoroughly to see whether it was in order or not. If there is any material omission or mistake, it may be returned to the policyholder or the assignee with a covering letter giving instructions as to the corrections to be made in the assignment or nomination.

When a document is sent for correction, reminders should be sent every fortnight until the requirements are complied with. The policyholder should follow the instructions printed on the back of assignment or nomination.

NOMINATION

Nomination is the process of identifying a person to receive the policy money in the event of the death of the Policyholder. Nomination can be done at the beginning of the Policy by giving details of nominee in the proposal form. However, if the nomination is not given at the beginning, the policyholder can give it at a later date. For that purpose a prescribed form is to be filled up and nomination can be endorsed on Policy Bond.

Change in Nomination

Change of nomination can be done by the policy holder any time during the term of the policy and any number of times he wants to. Procedure of nomination is same every time.

Withdrawal of nomination

Nomination can be withdrawn by the policy holder without giving prior notice to the nominee.

Nomination can be done only by a policyholder who has attained majority and on a policy on his life. Under Nomination, the Nominee gets only the right to receive the policy money in the event of the death of the Policyholder.

Death of the Nominee If the nominee dies and the policyholder is still surviving then the nomination would be ineffective. If Nominee dies after the death of the Policyholder but before receiving policy money, then also Nomination becomes ineffective and only the legal heirs of the policyholder can claim money.

Nomination at a later date After the policy is prepared and issued and if no Nomination has been given the assured can give the nomination only by an endorsement on the policy itself. A nomination is not required to be stamped. Nomination in favour of a stranger cannot be given as there is no insurable interest involved in that case. For nomination in favour of wife and children, specific names of wife and children should be given.

Successive Nominee

Where it is mentioned in nomination that the policy money should be paid to "Nominee A failing him to Nominee B whom failing to Nominee C, etc.", such nomination is called successive nomination.

Such nomination would be in favour of one individual in the order mentioned. All such Nomination would mean that if Nominee A were dead at the time in question the Nominee B would take the whole amount and that if both Nominees A and

B were then dead then Nominee C would take the whole amount and so on.

A Minor Nominee

In view of the Insurance (Amendment Act) 1950, the Life Assured has the right, where a nominee is a minor, to appoint any person as the Appointee to receive the moneys secured by the policy in the event of the assured's death during minority of the nominee.

The person so appointed will not be a guardian of the minor Nominee's power will be limited to the right to receive the policy money in the event of the assured's death during the minority of the Nominee.

The appointment must be a major. The appointment of Appointee must be communicated to the insurance company. So his name can be registered with the company. The appointment can be cancelled or changed by the life assured any time before the maturity of the policy.

ASSIGNMENT

Assignment is a means whereby the right and title under a policy gets transferred from assignor to assignee. Assignor is the policyholder who transfers the title and assignee is the person who gets the title of the policy from the assignor. Assignment can be made either by endorsement on the policy or on a separate paper duly stamped. Assignor must be a major. Assignment must be in writing and assignor's signature along with a witness is required. Notice of assignment should be submitted to the insurer by the assignor. Assignment can be of two types:

1. Absolute Assignment: In which all the rights, title and interest of the assignor in the policy passes on to the assignee without the possibility of cancellation of the same.
2. Conditional Assignment: In which the assignor and the assignee may agree that in case specified event or events

happen, the assignment would be cancelled or ineffective in part or as a whole.

Impact of Assignment

In assignment, assignor gives all the rights over the policy to the assignee that becomes the owner of the policy. The assignee has the right to reassign that policy.

In the event of Death of the Assignee

If the assignment is conditional assignment and the assignee dies, the assignment becomes ineffective and all the rights and title of the policy goes back to the life assured if he is alive. If the life assured is not surviving, the benefit goes back to the life assured's nominee.

In case of absolute assignment, if the assignee dies, all the rights entitled of the policy are given to legal heirs of the assignee.

Cancellation of Assignment

An assignment once executed cannot be cancelled, however, if an assignee during the term of the policy reassigns the interest and title of the policy to the previous assignor such reassignment will result in cancellation of assignment and the benefits of the policy go back to the original assignor.

Procedures of Assignment

A standard form of Assignment is issued to the policyholder who wants to effect an assignment of his policy. Necessary instructions are there for executing the assignment which is then registered by the insurance company. Points to be checked by the insurance company for affecting assignment:

(1) Check whether the assignment is executed on the Policy or on a separate paper and if it is executed on a separate paper that the paper is adequately stamped. If it is unstamped or inadequately stamped inform the assignor and get it corrected.

(2) Check whether notice of assignment is received from the assignor; if the notice is not received or it is defective, inform the assignor.

(3) Check the signatures of assignor affixed to the assignment and notice with the specimen of his signature in the proposal papers to see that they tally. If the signature differs then for writing letter to the person concerned, inform the assignor.

(4) If the assignment is executed on a separate paper, ensure that the paper should be stamped, in accordance with the stamp regulations.

(5) Check that the data and place of execution on Assignment are mentioned. If they are not mentioned the assignment may be registered, if otherwise in order, but while returning the Assignment to the party concerned he should be asked to have the necessary particulars inserted in the Assignment under the Assignor's.

If the assignment is in order and that the notice there of has been duly received the particulars of assignment must be entered in the space provide for the purpose in the Policy Ledger Sheet under the heading "Nominations and Assignments". Also the appropriate rubber stamp is affixed at the foot of assignment write the date on which the assignment and the notice are received.

ALTERATIONS

After issue of a Policy, the Policy holder desires an alteration in the terms thereof to suit his convenience, e.g., an alteration in the mode of payment of premiums, Plan of Assurance, reduction in the premium-paying period, etc. An alteration may be allowed provided the policy is in force and has not become fully paid up. It is stated in the prospectus that no alteration from one class of Assurance to another subject to a lower scale of premium is permissible.

However, an alteration from the with profits Limited Payment plan to the with profits Endowment Assurance Plan with premiums payable for a term not exceeding the original premium-paying term will be allowed even if the premium payable on alteration is lower. Alterations from certain Classes of Assurance to certain other Classes are not allowed at all.

Frequently requested alterations by the policyholders are:

(1) Alteration in Name;

(2) Reduction in the Sum Assured;

(3) Adding Double Accident Benefit and Extended Disability Benefit.

(4) Alteration in Class or Term;

(5) Removal of an extra premium;

(6) Alteration in the Mode of Payment of Premiums;

(7) Alteration form Without Profits Plan to With Profits Plan;

(8) Correction in Policies;

No alteration will be permitted within one year of the commencement of the policy, except the few cases like:

(1) Compulsory alterations such as alteration in name, correction in policies, alteration in currency of payment of policy moneys and alterations age proving higher or lower than that stated at the time of proposal.

(2) Requests for addition of Double Accident Benefit, Extended Disability Benefit.

(3) Change in the mode of payment of premium to 'monthly' so as to bring the policy under Salary Saving Scheme or to finance the same from Provident Fund Account.

(4) Conversion of ordinary policies to those issued under Married Women's Property Act, as provided in the Manual on the subject of 'Married Women's Property Act'.

ALTERATION FEE

"Alteration fee" is required in the following cases;

(1) Alteration in the mode of payment whereby there is an increase in the frequency of payment of premium installments, e.g., alteration from yearly to half-yearly, quarterly or monthly, etc.;

(2) When policyholder wants to add Double Accident Benefit or Extended Disability Benefit after the issue of the Policy and such Benefit is not granted from the commencement;

(3) Reduction in the Sum Assured;

(4) When policyholder wants to add Premium Waiver Benefit under a Child Deferred Annuity policy after its issue and such Benefit is not granted form the commencement.

No fee is required for Alterations of the following types:

(1) Where the alteration should necessarily be made in age of the policyholder, as age stated in the policy is not correct. The age stated in the policy may be understated or overstated.

(2) Where policyholder wants to reduce the frequency of payment of installments of premiums in the year.

(3) Where change or correction is required in the name of the assured, nominee, assignee etc., in the policy.

Loan on Policy

Most of the insurance companies give facility to the policyholders to get loans on Life Insurance policies according to rules. The policyholder can apply for a loan in a prescribed form and has to give policy bond along with the completed form.

The loan amount that the policyholder can get is calculated according to surrender value of the policy at the time of taking the loan. Rate of interest charged on the loan by the insurance company may vary from time to time and may depend upon the rules of the insurance company. For loan the policy should be assigned absolutely in favour of the insurance company.

Repayment of Loan

The life assured can repay the loan either in full or in part anytime during the term of the policy. If the loan is not repaid during the term of the policy, the amount of loan and its interest will be subtracted from the claimed amount on the policy and the balance will be given to the policyholder.

When a loan is granted, it is entered with the particulars in the Policy Register Sheet of the insurance company. When the policyholder repays the loan in full or part, the particulars are entered in the Policy Ledger Sheet. Separate loan bond should be made and given to the policyholder for the purpose of granting more than one loans. However, only one cheque may be issued for all the loans.

Generally, the loans are not allowed for the following policies.

1. Immediate Annuity and Deferred Annuity Policies.
2. Children's Deferred Assurance policies during deferment period.
3. Janata Policies.
4. Where the assured or the assignee is incompetent to contract.
5. Where policies carry conditions or endorsements taking away the right of raising loans from the assured.
6. Policies issued under Married Women's Property Act.
7. Where the policies are lost or damaged.

SURRENDER VALUE

If the insured is unwilling or unable to pay the premium of the policy, he may surrender the policy and ask for its surrender value. Surrender value is the cash value payable by the insurance on voluntary termination of the policy contract by the life assured before the expiry of the term of the policy. Surrender value depends on the type of policy and number of premia paid. A policy can be surrendered only when the premia is paid for the three years.

PAID UP VALUE

When a policyholder wants to terminate the policy, he may convert the same into paid-up policy. In this case, the amount of paid-up value is payable to the insured only after the full term (maturity) of the policy. The option of converting the policy into paid up policy and stop paying the further premiums can be taken only if the policy has been in force for at least two years.

6

ESSENTIAL FEATURE OF INSURANCE CONTRACT

INTRODUCTION

The purchasers of Insurance have to enter into a contract, where by one party (insured) agrees to pay to other party (insurer) a certain sum of money, determined on the happening of a certain event in consideration of a certain sum of money caned Premium. Such a contract is known as "Insurance Contract". Like any other contract, Insurance contract are also governed by the provisions of the law of contract as laid down in The Indian Contract Act, 1872. Therefore they have to fulfill the essential features of a valid contract. The essentials of a valid contract have been discussed earlier.

Life Insurance Corporation Act, 1956

An Act to provide for the nationalization of life insurance business in India by transferring all such business to a Corporation established for the purpose and to provide for the regulation and control of the business of the Corporation and for matters connected there with or incidental thereto.

Some of the important provisions are as follows: —

1. Short title and commencement. —

(1) This Act maybe called the Life Insurance Corporation Act, 1956

(2) It shall come into force on such date as the Central Government may, by Notifications in the Official Gazette, appoint. Definitions: In this Act, unless the context otherwise requires,

(1) "Appointed day," means the date on which the Corporation is established under Section 3;

(2) "Composite insurer "means an insurer carrying on in addition to controlled business any other kind of insurance business;

(3) "Controlled business" means—

(i) In the case of any insurer specified in sub-clause (a) or sub-clause (b) of clause (9) of section 2 of the Insurance Act and carrying on life insurance business—

(a) all his business, if he carries on no other class of insurance business;

(b) all the business appertaining to his life insurance business, if he carries on any other class of insurance business also;

(c) all his business if his certificate of registration under the Insurance Act in respect of general insurance business stands wholly cancelled for a period of more than six months on the 19th day of January, 1956.

(ii) in the case of any other insurer specified in clause (9) ofsection2 of the Insurance Act and carrying on life insurance business—

(a) all his business in India, if he carries on no other class of insurance business in India;

(b) all the business appertaining to his life insurance business in India, if he carries on any other class of insurance business also in India;

(c) all his business in India if he certificate of registration under the Insurance Act in respect of general insurance business in India stands wholly cancelled for a period of more than six months on the 19th day of January, 1956.

Explanation

An insurer is said to carry on no class of insurance business other than life insurance business,if in addition to life insurance business, he carries on only capital redemption business or annuity certain business or both;and the expression" business appertaining to his life insurance business" in sub-clause (i) and (ii) shall be construed accordingly; (iii) in the case of a provident society, as defined in section 65 of the Insurance; Act, all its business; (iv) in the case of the Central Government or a State Government, all life insurance business carried on by it, subject to the exceptions specified in section44;

(4) "Corporation" means the Life Insurance Corporation of India established under section 3;

(5) "Insurance Act" means the Insurance Act, 1938(4of1938);

(6) "Insurer" means an insurer as defined in the Insurance Act who carries on life insurance business in India and includes the Government and a provident society as defined in section65 of the Insurance Act;

(7) "Member" means a member of the Corporation;

(8) "Prescribed" means prescribed by rules made under this Act;

(9) "Tribunal" means a Tribunal constituted under section17 and having jurisdiction in respect of any matter under the rules made under this Act;

(10) All other words and expressions used herein but not defined and defined in the Insurance Act shall have the meanings respectively assigned to them in that Act.

Establishment and incorporation of Life Insurance Corporation of India.—

(1) With effect from such date as the Central Government may, by notification in the Official Gazette, appoint, there shall be established a Corporation called the Life Insurance Corporation of India.

(2) The Corporation shall be a body corporate having perpetual succession and a common seal with power subject to the provisions of this Act, to acquire, hold and dispose of property, and may by its name sue and be sued.

Constitution of the Corporation

(1) The Corporation shall consist of such number of persons not exceeding 2 as the Central Government may think fit to appoint thereto and one of them shall be appointed by the Central Government to be the Chairman there of.

(2) Before appointing a person to be a member, the Central Government shall satisfy itself that person will have no such financial or other interest as is likely to affect prejudicially the exercise or performance by him of his functions as a member, and the Central Government shall also satisfy itself from time to time with respect to every member that he has no such interest; and any person who is, or whom the Central Government proposes to appoint and who has consented to be, a member shall, whenever required by the Central Government so to do, furnish to it such information as the Central Government considers necessary for the performance of its duties under this sub-section.

(3) A member who is in anyway directly or indirectly interested in a contract made or proposed to be made by the Corporation shall as soon as possible after the relevant circumstances have come to his knowledge, disclose the nature of his interest to the Corporation and the member shall not take part in any deliberation or discussion of the Corporation with respect to that contact.

Capital of the Corporation.—

(1) The original capital of the Corporation shall be five crores of rupees provided by the Central Government after due appropriation made by Parliament bylaw for the purpose, and the terms and conditions relating to the provision of such capital shall be such as maybe determined by the Central Government.

(2) The Central Government may, on the recommendation of the Corporation, reduce the capital of the Corporation to such extent and in such manner as the Central Government may determine.

Functions of the Corporation

1) Subject, to the rules, if any, made by the Central Government in this behalf, it shall be the general duty of the Corporation to carry on life insurance business, whether in or outside India, and the Corporation shall so exercise its powers under this Act as to secure that life insurance business is developed to the best advantage of the community.

2) Without prejudice to the generality of the provisions contained in sub-section (1) but subject to the other provisions contained in this Act, the Corporation shall have power —

   (a) To carryon capital redemption business, annuity certain business or reinsurance business in so far as such re insurance business appertains to life insurance business;

   (b) Subject to the rules, if any, made by the Central Government in this behalf, to invest the funds of the Corporation in such manner as the Corporation may think fit and to take all such steps as may be necessary or expedient for the protection or realization of any investment; including the taking over of and administering any property offered as security for the investment until a suitable opportunity arises for its disposal;

(c) To acquire, hold and dispose of any property for the purpose of its business;

(d) To transfer the whole or any part of the life insurance business carried on outside India to any other person or persons, if in the interest of the Corporation it is expedient so to do;

(e) To advance or lend money upon the security of any movable property or otherwise;

(f) To borrow or raise any money in such manner and upon such security as the Corporation may think fit;

(g) To carry on either by itself or through any subsidiary any other business in any case where such other business was being carried on by a subsidiary of an insurer whose controlled business has been transferred to and invested in the Corporation under this Act;

(h) to carry on any other business which may seen to the Corporation to be capable of being conveniently carried on in connection with its business and calculated directly or indirectly to render profitable the business of the corporation;

(i) to do all such things as maybe incidental or conducive to the proper exercise of any of the powers of the Corporation. In the discharge of any of its functions the Corporation shall act so far as maybe on business principles.

Power to Impose Conditions, etc.

(1) In entering into any arrangement, under section 6, with any concern, the Corporation may impose such conditions as it may think necessary or expedient for protecting the interest of the Corporation and for securing that the accommodation granted by it is put to the best use by the concern.

(2) Where any arrangement entered into by the Corporation under section 6 with any concern provides for the appointment by the Corporation of one or more directors of such concern, such provision and any appointment of directors made in pursuance there of shall be valid and effective notwithstanding anything to the contrary contained in the Companies Act, 1956 (1 of1956),or in any other law for the time being in force or in the memorandum, articles of association or any other instrument relating to the concern, and any provision regarding share, qualification, age limit, number of directorships, removal from office of Directors and such like conditions contained in any such law or instrument aforesaid, shall not apply to any director appointed by the Corporation in pursuance of the arrangement as aforesaid.

(3) Any director appointed as aforesaid shall-

(a) Hold office during the pleasure o f the Corporation any maybe removed or substituted by any person by order in writing by the Corporation;

(b) Not incur any obligation or liability by reason only of his being a director or for anything done or omitted to be done in good faith in the discharge of his duties as a director or anything in relation thereto;

(c) Not be liable to retirement by rotation and shall not be taken into account for computing the number of directors liable to such retirement.

Offices, Branches and Agencies

(1) The central office of the Corporation shall be at such place as the Central Government may, by notification in he Official Gazette, specify.

(2) The Corporation shall establish a zonal office at each of the following places, namely, Bombay, Calcutta, Delhi, Kanpur and Madras, and, subject to the previous

approval of the Central Government, may establish such other zonal offices as it thinks fit.

(3) The territorial limits of each zone shall be such as may be specified by the Corporation.

(4) There may be established as many divisional offices and branches in each zone as the Zonal Manager thinks fit.

Committees of the Corporation

(1) The Corporation may entrust the general superintendence and direction of its affairs and business to an Executive Committee consisting of not more than five of its members and the Executive Committee may exercise all powers and do all such acts and things as may be delegated to it by the Corporation.

(2) The Corporation may also constitute an Investment Committee for the purpose of advising it in matters relating to the investment of its funds, and the Investment Committee shall consist of not more than eight members of whom not less than four shall be members of the Corporation and the remaining members shall be persons (whether members of the Corporation or not) who have special knowledge and experience in financial matters, particularly, matters relating to investment of funds.

(3) The Corporation may constitute such other Committees as it may thin fit for the purpose of discharging such of its functions as maybe delegated to them.

Funds of the Corporation

The Corporation shall have its own fund and all receipts of the Corporation shall be credited thereto and all payments of the Corporation shall be made there from. Audit.—

(1) The accounts of the Corporation shall be audited by auditors duly qualified to act as auditors of companies under the law for the time being in force relating to

companies, and the auditors shall be appointed by the Corporation with the previous approval of the Central Government and shall receive such remuneration from the Corporation as the Central Government may fix.

(2) Every auditor in the performance of his duties shall have at all reasonable times access to the books, accounts and other documents of the Corporation.

(3) The auditors shall submit their report to the Corporation and shall also forward a copy of their report to the Central Government.

Annual Report of activities of Corporation

The Corporation shall, as soon as may be, after the end of each financial year, prepare and submit to the Central Government in such form as maybe prescribed a report giving an account of its activities during the previous financial year, and the report shall also give an account of the activities, if any, which are likely to be undertaken by the Corporation in the next financial year.

General Insurance Contract, 1972

Although Life Insurancc was nationalized as early as 1956, general insurance business continued to be in the private sector right up to 1969. In that year the Government imposed strict social control on General Insurance Companies. This was a prelude to nationalization of General of General Insurance Business. With effect from 13th May, 1971 under the provisions of General Insurance (Emergency Provisions) Act, 1971 the Government of India took over the management of all General Insurance Companies operating in India whether they belonged to Indian or non-Indian shareholders.

Subsequently, the General Insurance (Emergency Provisions) Amendment Act, 1971 was passed withdrawing certain rights of the Directors and Members of the Companies, which they were enjoying under the Companies Act. General Insurance (Nationalization) Act, 1972 shortly followed and with effect from 2nf January, 1973 the provisions of the Act became effective. The functions of the Corporation are enumerated in Section18 of the Act, some of are as follows:

Functions of Corporation –

(1) The functions of the Corporation shall include:-

(a) The carrying on of any part of the general insurance business, if it thinks it desirable to do so;

(b) Aiding, assisting and advising the acquiring companies in the matter of setting up of standards of conduct and sound practice in general insurance business and in the matter of rendering efficient services to holders of policies of general insurance;

(c) Advising the acquiring companies in the matter of the controlling their expenses including the payment of commission and other expenses.

(d) Advising the acquiring companies in the matter of the investment of their funds;

(e) Issuing directions to acquiring companies in relation to the conduct of general insurance business.

(2) In issuing any directions under sub-section (1), the Cooperation shall keep in mind the desirability of encouraging composition amongst the acquiring companies as far as possible in order to render their services more efficient."

Functions of acquiring companies:-

(1) Subject to the rules, if any, made by the Central Government in this behalf and to its memorandum and articles of association, it shall be the duty of every acquiring company to carry on general insurance business.

(2) Each acquiring company shall so function under this Act as to secure that general insurance business is developed to the best of the community.

(3) In the discharge of any of its functions, each acquiring company shall act so far as may be on business principles and where any directions have been issued by the Corporation shall be guided by such directions.

(4) For the removal of doubts it is hereby declared that the Corporations and any acquiring company may, subject to the rules, if any, made by the Central Government in this behalf, "enter into such contracts of reinsurance treaties as it may think fit for the protection of its interests".

Under Sec. 35, The Central Government may by notification specify the application of the provision of the Insurance Act with such modifications as is deemed necessary to the Corporation and the acquiring companies. The Central Government is also empowered to make rules to carry out the provisions of the Act and such rules may provide for:

(a) Manner in which the profits and other moneys received by the Corporation may be dealt with'

(b) The conditions subject to which the Corporation and the acquiring companies shall carry on general insurance business;

(c) The terms and conditions subject to which any re-insurance contract or treaties may be entered into;

(d) Form and manner in which any notice or application may be made to the Central Government;

(e) The reports which may be called for by the Central Government from the Corporation and acquiring companies; and

(f) Any other matter which is required to be or may be prescribed.

THE INSURANCE ACT, 1938

Earlier to the Insurance Act, 1938, the insurance business was carried by the insurance companies in accordance with the principles of the Company Law, 1913. When the business started growing, the need for an independent law to regulate the insurance business was noticed and a separate Act, the Insurance Act, 1938 was legislated.

The Act was used for all purposes relating to both life and general insurance businesses and their regulations. With regards to general insurance, this Act is being used to regulate the marine insurance, fire insurance and other insurances. Further growth of business has made it complex and more legal provisions were required to regulate it. The Marine Insurance Act, 1963, Public Liability Insurance Act, 1991, Insurance Regulatory and Development Authority Act, 1999 and regulations made by the IRDA are some of the legislations that govern the insurance business.

Short Title, Extent and Commencement

1. (1) This Act may be called Insurance Act, 1938.

(2) It extends to the whole of India.

(3) It shall come into force on such date3 as the Central Government may, by Notification in the Official Gazette, appoint in this behalf.

Definitions.

2. In this Act, unless there is anything repugnant in the subject or context,-

(1) "Authority" means the Insurance Regulatory and Development Authority established under sub-section (1) of section 3 of the Insurance Regulatory and Development Authority Act, 1999;

(2) "Policy-holder" includes a person to whom the whole of the interest of the policy-holder in the policy is assigned once and for all, but does not include an assignee thereof whose interest in the policy is infeasible or is for the time being subject to any condition;

(3) "Approved securities," means-

(i) Government securities and other securities charged on the revenue of the Central Government or of the Government of a State or guaranteed fully as regards principal and interest by the Central Government or the Government of any State;

(ii) debentures or other securities for money issued under the authority of any Central Act or Act of a State Legislature by or on behalf of a port trust or municipal corporation or city improvement trust in any Presidency-town;

(iii) shares of a corporation established by law and guaranteed fully by the Central Government or the Government of a State as to the repayment of the principal and the payment of the divided;

(iv) securities issued or guaranteed fully as regards principal and interest by the Government of any Part B State and specified as approved securities for the purposes of this Act by the Central Government by notification in the Official Gazette; and

(4) "Auditor" means a person qualified under the Chartered Accountants Act, 1949 (38 of 1949), to act as an auditor of companies;

(4A) "Banking company" and "company" shall have the meanings respectively assigned in them in clauses (c) and (d) of sub-section (1) of Section 5 of the Banking Companies Act, 1949 (10 of 1949);

(5) "Certified" in relation to any copy or translation of a document required to be furnished by or on behalf of an insurer or a provident society as defined in Part III means certified by a principal officer of 6Esuch insurer or provident society to be a true copy or a correct translation, as the case may be;

(5A) "Chief agent" means a person who, not being a salaried employee of an insurer, in consideration of any commission-

(i) Performs any administrative and organizing functions for the insurer, and

(ii) Procures life insurance business for the insurer by employing or causing to be employed insurance agents on behalf of the insurer;

(5-B) "Controller of Insurance" means the officer appointed by the Central Government under section 2B to exercise all the powers, discharge the functions and performs the duties of the Authority under this Act or the Life Insurance Corporation Act, 1956 (31 of 1956) or the General Insurance Business (Nationalization) Act, 1972 (57 of 1972) or the Insurance Regulatory and Development Authority Act, 1999;]

(6) "Court" means the principal Civil Court of original jurisdiction in a district and includes the High Court in exercise of its ordinary original civil jurisdiction;

(6A) "Fire insurance business" means the business of effecting, otherwise than incidentally to some other class of insurance business, contracts of insurance against loss by or incidental to fire or other occurrence customarily included among the risks insured against in fire insurance Policies;

(6B) "General insurance business" means fire, marine or miscellaneous insurance business, whether carried on singly or in combination with one or more of them;

(7) "Government security" means a Government security as defined in the Public Debt Act, 1944 (18 of 1944);

(7A) "Indian insurance company" means any insurer being a company-

(a) which is formed and registered under the Companies Act, 1956 (1 of 1956);

(b) in which the aggregate holdings of equity shares by a foreign company, either by itself or through its subsidiary companies or its nominees, do not exceed twenty-six percent paid-up equity capital of such Indian insurance company;

(c) whose sole purpose is to carry on life insurance business or general insurance business or re-insurance business.

(8) "Insurance company" means any insurer being a company, association or partnership which may be wound up under the Indian Companies Act, 1913 (7 of 1913), or to which the Indian Partnership Act, 1932 (9 of 1932), applies;

(9) "Insurer" means-

(a) any individual or unincorporated body of individuals or body corporate incorporated under the law of any country other than India, carrying on insurance business not being a person specified in sub-clause (c) of this clause which-

(i) carries on that business in India, or

(ii) has his or its principal place of business or is domiciled in India, or

(iii) with the object of obtaining insurance business, employs a representative, or maintains a place of business, in India;

(b) any body corporate [not being a person specified in sub-clause (c) of this clause] carrying on the business of insurance, which is a body corporate incorporated under any law for the time being in force in India; or stands to any such body corporate in the relation of a subsidiary company within the meaning of the Indian Companies Act, 1913 (7 of 1913), as defined by sub-section (2) of section 2 of that Act, and

(c) any person who in India has a standing contract with underwriters who are members of the Society of Lloyd's whereby such person is authorized within the terms of such contract to issue protection notes, cover notes, or other documents granting insurance cover to others on behalf of the underwriters. But does not include a principal agent' chief agent, special agent' or an insurance agent or a provident society as defined in Part III;

(10) "Insurance agent" means an insurance agent licensed under Sec. 42 who receives agrees to receive payment by way of commission or other remuneration in consideration of his soliciting or procuring insurance business including business relating to the continuance, renewal or revival of policies of insurance;

(10A) "investment company" means a company whose principal business is the acquisition of shares, stocks debentures or other securities;

(10B) "Intermediary or insurance intermediary" shall have the meaning assigned to it in clause (f) of sub-section 2 of the Insurance Regulatory and Development Authority Act, 1999 (41 of 1999)

(11) "Life insurance business" means the business of effecting contracts of insurance upon human life, including any contract whereby the payment of money is assured on death (except death by accident only) or the happening of any

(12) "Manager" and "officer" have the meanings assigned to those expressions in clauses (9) and (11), respectively of Section 2 of the Indian Companies Act, 1913 (7 of 1913);

(13) "Managing agent" means a person, firm or company entitled to the management of the whole affairs of a company by virtue of an agreement with the company, and under the control and direction of the directors except to the extent, if any, otherwise provided for in the agreement, and includes any person, firm or company occupying such position by whatever name called.

Explanation. —If a person occupying the position of managing agent calls himself manager or managing director, he shall nevertheless be regarded as managing agent for the purposes of Sec. 32 of this Act;

(13A) "marine insurance business" means the business of effecting contracts of insurance upon vessels of any description, including cargoes, freights and other interests which may be legally insured, in or in relation to such vessels, cargoes and freights, goods, wares, merchandise and property of whatever description insured for any transit, by land or water, or both, and whether or not including warehouse risks or similar risks in addition or as incidental to such transit, and includes any other risks customarily included among the risks insured against in marine insurance policies;

(13B) "miscellaneous insurance business" means the business of effecting contracts of insurance which is not principally or wholly of any kind or kinds included in clause (6A), (11) and (13A);

(14) "Prescribed" means prescribed by rules made under this Act; and

(15) "Principal agent" means a person who, not being a salaried employee of an insurer, in consideration of any commission,—

(i) Performs any administrative and organizing functions for the insurer; and

(ii) Procures general insurance business whether wholly or in part by employing or causing to be employed insurance agents on behalf of the

(16) "Private company" and "public company" have the meanings respectively assigned to them in Clauses (13) and (13-A) of Sec. 2 of the Indian Companies Act, 1913 (7 of 1913);

(17) "Special agent" means a person who, not being a salaried employee of an insurer, in consideration of any commission, procures life insurance business for the insurer whether wholly or in part by employing or causing to be employed insurance agents on behalf of the insurer, but does not include a chief agent.

Appointment of Authority of Insurance

(1) If at any time, the Authority is superseded under sub-section (1) of section19 of the Insurance Regulatory and Development Authority Act, 1999, the Central Government may, by notification in the Official Gazette, appoint a person to be the Controller of Insurance till such time the Authority is reconstituted under subsection (3) of section 19 of that Act.

(2) In making any appointment under this section, the Central Government shall have due regard to the following considerations, namely, whether the person to be appointed has had experience in industrial, commercial or insurance matter and whether such person has actuarial qualifications. Requirements as to capital.

No insurer carrying on the business of life insurance, general insurance or re58 insurance in India on or after the commencement of the Insurance Regulatory and Development authority Act, 199, shall be registered unless he has,-

(i) a paid-up equity capital of rupees one hundred crores, in case of a person carrying on the business of life insurance or general insurance; or

(ii) a paid-up equity capital of rupees two hundred crores, in case of a person carrying on exclusively the business as a reinsurer: Provided that in determining the paid-up equity capital specified under clause (i) or clause (ii), the deposit to be made under section 7 and any preliminary expenses incurred in the formation and registration of the company shall be excluded:

Provided further that an insurer carrying on business of life insurance, general insurance or re-insurance in India before the commencement of the Insurance Regulatory and Development Authority Act, 1999 and who is required to be registered under this Act, shall have a paid-up equity capital in accordance with clause (i) and clause (ii), as the case may be, within sex months of the commencement of that Act.

Deposits

Every insurer shall, in respect of the insurance business carried on by him in India, deposit and keep deposited with the Reserve Bank of India in one of the offices in India of the Bank for and on behalf of the Central Government the amount hereafter specified, either in cash or in approved securities estimated at the market value of the securities on the day of deposit, or partly in cash and partly in approved securities so estimated:-

(a) in the case of life insurance business, a sum equivalent to one per cent of his total gross premium written direct in India in any financial year commencing after the 31st day of March, 2000, not exceeding rupees ten crores;

(b) in the case of general insurance business, a sum equivalent to three per cent of his total gross premium written in India, in any financial year commencing after the 31st day of March, 2000, not exceeding rupees ten crores;

(c) in the case of re-insurance business, a sum of rupees twenty crores Provided that, where the business done or to be done is marine insurance only and relates exclusively to country craft or its cargo or both, the amount to be deposited under this sub-section shall be one hundred thousand rupees only: Provided further that in respect of an insurer not having a share capital and carrying on only such insurance business as in the opinion of the Central Government is not carried on ordinarily by insurers under separate policies, the Central Government may, by notification under Official Gazette, order that the provisions of this sub-section shall apply to such insurer with the modification that instead of sum of rupees twenty lakhs or rupees ten lakhs, as the case may be, the deposit to be made by such insurer shall be such amount, being not less than one hundred and fifty thousand rupees, as may be specified in the said order.

Audit

The balance-sheet, profit and loss account, revenue account and profit and loss appropriation account of every insurer, in the case of an insurer specified in sub-clause (a)(ii) or sub-clause (b) of clause (9) of section 2 in respect of all insurance business transacted by him, and in the case of any other insurer in respect of the insurance business transacted by him in India, shall, unless they are subject to audit under the Indian Companies Act, 1913 (7 of 1913), be audited annually by an auditor, and the auditor shall in the audit of all such accounts have the powers of, exercise the functions vested in, and discharge the duties and be subject to the liabilities and penalties imposed on, auditors of companies by section 145 of the Indian Companies Act, 1913.

This Act not to apply to preparation of account, etc., for periods prior to this Act coming into force. Nothing in this Act shall apply to the preparation of accounts by an insurer and the audit and submission thereof in respect of any accounting year which has expired prior to the commencement of this Act, and notwithstanding the other provisions of this Act, such accounts shall be prepared, audited and submitted in accordance with the law in force immediately before the commencement of this Act.

Investment of Assets

(1) Every insurer shall invest and at all times keep invested assets equivalent to not less than the sum of-

(a) the amount of his liabilities to holders of life insurance policies in India on account of matured claims, and

(b) the amount required to meet the liability on policies of life insurance maturing for payment in India, less-

(i) the amount of premiums which have fallen due to the insurer on such policies but have not been paid and the days of grace for payment of which have not expired, and

(ii) any amount due to the insurer for loans granted on and within the surrender values of policies of life insurance maturing for payment in India issued by him or by an insurer whose business he has acquired and in respect of which he has assumed liability, in the manner following, namely, twenty-five per cent of the said sum in Government securities, a further sum equal to not less than twenty-five per cent of the said sum in Government securities or other approved securities and the balance in any of the approved investments specified in sub-section (1) of section 27A or, subject to the limitations, conditions and restrictions specified in sub-section (2) of that section, in any over investment.

(2) For the purposes of subsection (1),—

(a) the amount of any deposit made under section 7 or section 98 by the insurer in respect of his life insurance business shall be deemed to be assets invested or kept invested Government securities;

(b) The securities of, or guaranteed as to principal and interest by, the Government of the United Kingdom shall be regarded as approved securities other than Government securities for a period of four years from the commencement of the Insurance (Amendment) Act, 1950 (47 of 1950), in the manner and to the extent hereinafter specified, namely:—

(i) during the first year, to the extent of twenty-five per cent in value of the sum referred to in sub-section (1);

(ii) during the second year, to the extent of eighteen and three fourths per cent in value of the said sum;

(iii) during the third year, to the extent of twelve and a half per cent in value of the said sum; and

(iv) during the fourth year, to the extent of six and a quarter per cent in value of the said sum: Provided that, if the Authority so directs in any case, the securities specified in clause (b) shall be regarded as approved securities other than Government securities for a longer period than four years, but not exceeding six years in all and the manner in which and the extent to which the securities shall be so regarded shall be as specified in the direction;

(c) Any prescribed assets shall, subject to such conditions, if any, as may be prescribed, be deemed to be assets invested or kept invested in approved investments specified in sub-section (1) of section 27A.

(3) In computing the assets referred to in subsection (1),—

(a) any investment made with reference to any currency other than the Indian rupee which is in excess of the amount required to meet the liabilities of the insurer in India with reference to that currency, to the extent of such excess; and

(b) any investment made in the purchase of any immoveable property outside India or on the security of any such property, shall not be taken into account: Provided that nothing contained in this sub-section shall affect the operation of sub-section (2): Provided further that the Authority may, either generally or in any particular case, direct that any investment, whether made before or after the commencement of the Insurance (Amendment) Act, 1950 (47 of 1950), and whether made in or outside India, shall, subject to such conditions as may be imposed, be taken into account, in such manner as may be specified in computing the assets referred to in sub-section (1) and where any direction has been issued under this proviso copies thereof shall be laid before Parliament as soon as may be after it is issued.

(4) Where an insurer has accepted reassurance in respect of any policies of life insurance issued by another insurer and maturing for payment in India or has ceded reassurance to another insurer in respect of any such policies issued by himself, the sum referred to in subsection (1) shall be increased by the amount of the liability involved in such acceptance and decreased by the amount of the liability involved in such cession.

(5) The Government securities and other approved securities in which assets are under sub-section (1) to be invested and kept invested shall be held by the insurer free of any encumbrance, charge, hypothecation or lien.

(6) The assets required by this section to be held invested by an insurer incorporated or domiciled outside India shall, except to the extent of any part thereof which consists of foreign assets held outside India, be held in India and all such assets shall be held in trust for the discharge of the liabilities of the nature referred to in sub-section (1) and shall be vested in trustees resident in India and approved by the Authority, and the instrument of trust under this sub-section shall be executed by the insurer with the approval of the Authority and shall define the manner in which alone the subject-matter of the trust shall be dealt with.

Explanation.—This sub-section shall apply to an insurer-incorporated India whose share capital to the extent of one-third is owned by, or the members of whose governing body to the extent of one-third consists of, members domiciled elsewhere than in India.

Power to Appoint Staff

The Authority may appoint such staff, and at such places as it or he may consider necessary, for the scrutiny of the returns, statements and information furnished by insurers under this Act and generally to ensure the efficient performance of the functions of the Authority under this Act.

Registration of principal agents, chief agents and special agents

(1) The Authority or an officer authorized by it in this behalf shall in the prescribed manner and on payment of the prescribed fee, which shall not be more than twenty-five rupees for a principal agent or a chief agent and ten rupees for a special agent, register any person who makes an application to him in the prescribed manner if,—

(a) in the case of an individual, he does not suffer from any of the disqualifications mentioned in sub-section (4) of Section 42, or

(b) in the case of a company or firm, any of its directors or partners does not suffer from any of the said disqualifications, and a certificate to Act as a principal agent, chief agent or special agent, as the case may be, for the purpose of procuring insurance business shall be issued to him.

(2) A certificate issued under this section shall entitle the holder thereof to act as a principal agent, chief agent, or special agent, as the case may be, for any insurer.

(3) A certificate issued under this section shall remain in force for a period of twelve months only from the date of issue, but shall, on application made on this behalf, be renewed from year to year on production of a certificate from the insurer concerned that the provisions of clauses (2) and (3) of Part A of the Sixth Schedule in the case of a principal agent, the provisions of clauses (2) and (4) of Part B of the said Schedule in the case of a chief agent, and the provisions of clauses (2) and (3) of Part C of the said Schedule in the case of a special agent, have been complied with, and on payment of the prescribed fee, which shall not be more than twenty-five rupees, in the case of a principal agent or a chief agent, and ten rupees in the case of a special agent, and an additional fee of the prescribed amount not exceeding

five rupees by way of penalty, in cases where the application for renewal of the certificate does not reach the issuing authority before the date on which the certificate ceases to remain in force: Provided that, where the applicant is an individual, he does not suffer from any of the disqualifications mentioned in clauses (b) to (d) of sub-section (4) of section 42 and where the applicant is a company or a firm, any of its directors or partners does not suffer from any of the said disqualifications.

(4) Where it is found that the principal agent, chief agent or special agent being an individual is, or being a company or firm contains a director or partner who is suffering from any of the disqualifications mentioned in subsection (4) of section 42, without prejudice to any other penalty to which he may be liable, the Authority shall, and where a principal agent, chief agent or special agent has contravened any of the provisions of this Act may cancel the certificate issued under this section to such principal agent, chief agent or special agent.

(5) The authority which issued any certificate under this section may issue a duplicate certificate to replace a certificate lost, destroyed or mutilated on payment of the prescribed fee, which shall not be more than two rupees.

(6) Any person who acts as a principal agent, chief agent or special agent, without holding a certificate issued under this section to act as such, shall be punishable with fine which may extend to five hundred rupees, and any insurer or any person acting on behalf of an insurer, who appoints as a principal agent, chief agent or special agent any person not entitled to act as such or transacts any insurance business in India through any such person, shall be punishable with fine which may extend to one thousand rupees.

(7) Where the person contravening sub-section (6) is a company or a firm, then, without prejudice to any other

proceedings which may be taken against the company or firm, every director, manager, secretary or any other officer of the company, and every partner of the firm who is knowingly a party to such contravention shall be punishable with fine which may extend to five hundred rupees.

(8) The provisions of sub-sections (6) and (7) shall not take effect until the expiry of six months from the commencement of the Insurance (Amendment) Act, 1950.

(9) No insurer shall, on or after the commencement of the Insurance (Amendment) Act, 2002, appointment or transacts any insurance business in India through any principal agent, chief agent or special agent.

Regulation of Employment of Principal Agents

(1) No insurer shall, after the expiration of seven years from the commencement of the Insurance (Amendment) Act, 1950, appoint, or transact any insurance business in India, through a principal agent.

(2) Every contract between an insurer and a principal agent shall be in writing and the terms contained in Part A of the Sixth Schedule shall be deemed to be incorporated in, and form part of, every such contract.

(3) No insurer shall, after the commencement of the Insurance (Amendment) Act, 1950 (47 of 1950), appoint any person as a principal agent except in a presidency-town unless the appointment is by way of renewal of any contract subsisting at such commencement.

(4) Within sixty days of the commencement of the Insurance (Amendment) Act, 1950 (47 of 1950), every principal agent shall file with the insurer concerned a full list of insurance agents employed by him indicating the terms of the contract between the principal agent and each of such insurance agents, and, if any principal agent fails to file such a list within the period specified, any commission payable to such principal agent on premiums

received from the date of expiry of the said period of sixty days until the date of the filing of the said list shall, notwithstanding anything in any contract to the contrary, cease to be so payable.

(5) A certified copy of every contract as is referred to in sub-section (2) shall be furnished by the insurer to the Authority within thirty days of his entering into such contract, and intimation of any change in any such contract shall be furnished by the insurer with full particulars thereof to the Authority within thirty days of the making of any such change.

(6) If the commission due to any insurance agent in respect of any general insurance business procured by such agent is not paid by the principal agent for any reason, the insurer may pay the insurance agent the commission so due and recover the amount so paid from the principal agent concerned.

(7) Every contract as is referred to in sub-section (2), subsisting at the commencement of the Insurance (Amendment) Act, 1950 (47 of 1950), shall, with respect to terms regarding remuneration, be deemed to have been so altered as to be in accordance with the provisions of sub-section (4) of section 40A.

(8) If any dispute arises as to whether a person is or was a principal agent the matter shall be referred to the Authority, whose decision shall be final.

(9) Every insurer shall maintain a register in which the name and address of every principal agent appointed by him, the date of such appointment and the date, if any, on which the appointment ceased shall be entered.

Commission, Brokerage or Fee Payable to Intermediary or Insurance Intermediary

(1) No intermediary or insurance intermediary shall be paid or contract to be paid by way of commission, fee or as remuneration in any form, an amount exceeding thirty per cent of the premium payable as may be

specified by the regulations made by the Authority, in respect of any policy or policies effected through him: Provided that the Authority may specify different amounts payable by way of commission, fee or as remuneration to an intermediary or insurance intermediary or different classes of business of insurance.

(2) Without prejudice to the provisions contained in this Act, the Authority may, by the regulations made in this behalf, specify the requirements of capital, form of business and other conditions to act as an intermediary or insurance intermediary.

Register of Insurance Agents

Every insurer and every person who acting on behalf of an insurer employs insurance agents shall maintain a register showing the name and address of every insurance agent appointed by him and the date on which his appointment began and the date, if any, on which his appointment ceased.

IRDA ACT 1999

The Insurance Act, 1938 had provided for setting up of the Controller of Insurance to act as a strong and powerful supervisory and regulatory authority for insurance. Post nationalization, the role of Controller of Insurance diminished considerably in significance since the insurance companies were owned by the Government.

With the opening up of the insurance industry to the private sector, the need for a strong, independent and autonomous Insurance Regulatory Authority was felt. As the enacting of legislation would have taken time, the then Government constituted through a Government resolution an Interim Insurance Regulatory Authority pending the enactment of a comprehensive legislation. The Insurance Regulatory and Development Authority Act, 1999 is an act to provide for the establishment of an Authority to protect the interests of holders of insurance policies, to regulate, promote and ensure orderly growth of the insurance industry and for matters connected therewith or incidental thereto and further to amend the

Insurance Act, 1938, the Life Insurance Corporation Act, 1956 and the General insurance Business (Nationalization) Act, 1972 to end the monopoly of the Life Insurance Corporation of India (for life insurance business) and General Insurance Corporation and its subsidiaries (for general insurance business).

Extent and Commencement

- This Act may be called the Insurance Regulatory and Development Authority Act, 1999.
- The act extends to the whole of India and will come into force on such date as the Central Government may, by notification in the Official Gazette specify. Different dates may be appointed for different provisions of this Act.
- The Act has defined certain terms, some of the most important ones are as follows:-
- Appointed day means the date on which the Authority is established under the act.
- Authority means the established under this Act.

With effect from such date as the Central Government may, by notification, appoint the Insurance Regulatory and Develop is to be constituted. The Authority shall be a body corporate, having perpetual succession and a common seal with power, subject to the provisions of this Act, to acquire, hold and dispose of property, and to contract and can be sue or be sued in its own name. The head office of the Authority shall be at such place as the Central Government may decide from time to time and it may establish offices at other places in India.

7

INSURANCE SUPERVISION

INTRODUCTION

In reviewing the assessment findings, it was noted that several insurance supervisors also had supervisory responsibilities for pension systems, which were reviewed as part of the FSAP process. Whereas private pensions normally have limited implications for systemic liquidity (the potential exception being when banks act as fund managers and performance guarantees are required by law), they can have significant fiscal implications where government explicit or implicit guarantees are granted, and underfunding or investment subsidies are involved. The ICP does not specifically deal with pensions except to the extent that the insurance industry provides products that support the provision of pensions.

Guidance is lacking for the insurance supervisors who also oversee the pension system. Furthermore, there are no international standards for pension regulation and supervision, although some regional attempts have been made. However, in future FSAP work, it would be useful, in discussing the financial sector and the role of insurance, to identify and discuss the significance of the insurance and pensions benefits and the extent to which they could impact the resilience and development of the financial sector.

Difficulties in Carrying Out Assessments

Several factors have limited the efficacy of the assessment process thus far. Assessments were influenced by the changes made in the ICP and the development of various standards underlying the principles. The shortcomings in the ICP and the Methodology, the measurement problems in terms of differing accounting and actuarial practices, and the resources required to actually go beyond assessing formal rules to issues and implementation and enforcement, have also constrained a uniform approach toward these assessments.

In this regard, the IAIS self-assessment program is a welcome step and should facilitate the assessment under the FSAP, both in terms of the preparedness of the supervisory authorities and in fulfilling the pre-FSAP information requirements. In addition, further work is required on the ICP and the standards that are linked to these principles, so that supervisory systems can be strengthened and assessments can be more uniform.

Future Work

There are two key future tasks, the first of which is to provide feedback and provide ongoing support to the IAIS as the ICP evolves in light of emerging experience. Specifically, the areas identified for further improvements in the ICP should be considered by the IAIS when the re-examination of the supervisory principles is taken up in 2002. Their use in providing indications of macroeconomic and financial vulnerabilities also needs strengthening. The Bank and Fund staff would provide all possible assistance to the IAIS in this task.

The second task is to continue developing the Methodology (with the IAIS) and the templates to ensure that the ICP assessments are appropriate and relevant, and carried out in a consistent manner, allowing for preconditions and the stage of development of the insurance market. In addition, there is growing evidence that many member countries will be seeking post-FSAP advice and assistance to upgrade their insurance regulatory framework and supervisory capacity.

Finally, preparation of comprehensive and objective self-assessments by supervisory authorities, in advance of the FSAP assessment, would also help the assessment process. In particular, it will facilitate a more in-depth assessment of the strengths and weaknesses of insurance supervision, with enhanced focus on implementation, enforcement, and cross-sectoral issues. The Bank and the Fund are examining opportunities to work with the IAIS in running training programs for both FSAP assessors and country-level self-assessors. Progressively, with changes in the regulatory and supervisory guidance from the IAIS, the tools available for the FSAP will improve, thus enhancing the objectivity and completeness of the assessments of the insurance systems of member countries.

Organization of an Insurance Supervisor (ICP 1): The insurance supervisor of a jurisdiction must be organized so that it is able to accomplish its primary task, i.e., to maintain effective, fair, safe, and stable insurance markets for the benefit and protection of policyholders. It should, at any time, be able to carry out this task effectively in accordance with the Insurance Core Principles.

Licensing and Changes in Control (ICPs 2, 3): Companies wishing to underwrite insurance in the domestic insurance market should be licensed and the insurance supervisor should review changes in the control of companies that are licensed in the jurisdiction.

Corporate Governance and Internal Controls (ICPs 4, 5): It is desirable that standards, which deal with corporate governance, be established in the jurisdiction. The supervisor should be able to review the internal controls and require the board of directors to provide suitable prudential oversight.

Prudential Rules (ICPs 6, 7, 8, 9, 10): Insurance companies should meet prudential standards established to limit or manage the amount of risk that they retain. Standards should be established in the areas of assets, liabilities, capital adequacy and solvency, derivatives and "off-balance sheet" items, and reinsurance.

Market Conduct (ICP 11): Insurance supervisors should ensure that insurers and intermediaries exercise the necessary knowledge, skills, and integrity in dealing with their customers.

Monitoring and On-Site Inspection (ICPs 12, 13): Insurance supervisors should get the information they need to properly form an opinion on the financial strength of the operations of each insurance company in their jurisdiction.

Sanctions (ICP 14): Insurance supervisors must have the power to take remedial action where problems involving licensed companies are identified.

Cross-Border Business Operations (ICP 15): The insurance supervisor should ensure that: no foreign insurance establishment escapes supervision; all insurance establishments of international insurance groups and international insurers are subject to effective supervision; the creation of a cross-border insurance establishment is subject to consultation between host and home supervisors; and foreign insurers providing insurance cover on a cross-border services basis are subject to effective supervision.

Coordination and Cooperation (ICP 16): In order to share relevant information with other insurance supervisors, adequate and effective communication should be developed and maintained.

Confidentiality (ICP 17): All insurance supervisors should be subject to professional secrecy constraints in respect of information obtained in the course of their activities.

This low affordable life insurance piece of writing desires to give you the information you have to know, to believe that you‘ve a set understanding on the branch of learning. It’s a new year, and along with that you make some New Year’s resolutions. For most individuals, these New Year’s resolutions will incorporate one or two things involving financial preparation.

But, do your New Year’s resolutions include covering you and your relatives with reasonably priced term online life coverage? If you do not own a policy plan by now, or even if you do have one, it is necessary to review your lives insurance coverage requisites. Unfortunately, many people will find themselves without sufficient online life insurance coverage and might be reassured to discover that this area of their financial portfolio can be among the simplest and most reasonably priced to remedy.

The good thing about term on line lifetime insurance, in addition to its reasonable cost, is that you can pick a policy plan that corresponds to your needs at this particular time in your life, and then you can study your needs at the time the interval you've decided on is expired.

Various periods of life necessitate specific insurance coverage levels. Check out the things you're facing in this upcoming year; did you have any life-altering developments that may require a different kind of coverage? Did you wed, have kids, acquire a home, go through a divorce, retire, get a sizable promotion or a new position (or any other fiscal windfall)? These are just a few of the life changes that usually call for a different kind of lifetime coverage cover.

Analysis shows that over twenty-five per cent of United States homes lack any member with online life coverage. Furthermore, the almost three-quarters of us who have living insurance coverage don't have the right amount of coverage levels for the part of life we've reached. Many may not understand that term online lifetime coverage has become so reasonably priced. There is heavy competition now among insurance companies wanting to insure you, and that competition translates into cheap, viable costs if you do a little comparative shopping.

One more detail to clarify is that whereas some consumers might understand they are able to pay for life assurance while they are young, many may not understand that older American citizens can generally procure affordable term living ins also. Experts indicate that in the previous couple of years, many more seniors have been acquiring term permanent life insurance. Let's take a look at a specific instance, that of a fit, 60-year-old gentleman trying to obtain a 10-year, hundred thousand dollar policy. This retired man may be able to buy a policy plan for as low as Rs.34.02 every month. Hardly the hundreds of dollars some consumers presume this might cost!

In addition, research shows American consumers are beginning to live longer, and this can and probably will bring down premiums for all customers, including older people. Research shows that in excess of 49,000 individuals nationally are over one hundred years of age, raised significantly from just ten years previous. According to United States Census data, the amount of persons who live to a hundred or more figures to increase by a hundred percent each decade, and by the year 2035, the 70-plus age range will be more than doubled.

What does this mean for your lifetime insurance rates? Well not only is prolonged life and quality fitness nice news for U.S. older people from a quality-of-living point of view, it is also decent news from a lifetime coverage perspective. Insurance coverage groups will be producing new actuarial tables that involve new mortality levels within the next five or six years, a lot of them even sooner.

Actuarial and life-expectancy tables are used by life coverage associations to figure the likelihood of death by a particular age. In other words, they convey to on line life assurance agencies the amount of time you are presumed to live on average based on your age and your gender.

For the only time in more than 2 decades, the American Academy of Actuaries has adjusted the table to indicate America's trend in the direction of existing longer. Expanded lives mean the mortality and expenses you remit for coverage should be lessened, which should thus lower your coverage premiums. Some insurance groups are pronouncing that the adjusted actuarial tables will allow them to drop their fees by up to 30 per cent once they are accepted.

One more valuable point to bear in mind is that people should study a variety of term lengths and amounts. You may just be stunned by the difference in personal expenses between a decade-long policy plan and a twenty-year policy plan, or between a 20-year policy and a twenty-five- or 30-year policy plan. We all ought to choose to ensure that we are adequately insured with online lifetime insure. Study costs on line today, and observe exactly how reasonably priced term lives ins could be.

INSURER'S OBLIGATIONS

The insurer's obligation to pay a claim is perhaps the most common issue in insurance disputes. The insurer's obligation to pay a claim depends on certain factors, like the circumstances surrounding the loss and the precise coverage of the insurance policy.

Normally a court chooses the most acceptable interpretation of the obligation if a disagreement arises over the words of the policy document. In fact to protect the insured, an incontestability clause is included in many insurance contracts. This clause denies the insurer the right to contest the validity of the contract after a specified period of time.

INSURED'S COMPLIANCE

If the insured party had hidden or distorted a material fact in the policy application the insurance company is within its rights to deny or cancel coverage. On the other hand if an application appears to have the potential for high risk of loss for the insurance company, it may reject the application or alternately offer a very high premium.

If an insured defaults in paying his premiums, the insurer may cancel the policy. Also if the insured intentionally caused the loss or damage the insurer can refuse to pay any claim for the same.

It may so happen that the insurer may knows that it can withdraw a policy or deny a claim, but conveys to the insured that it has willingly given up this right. In such circumstances the insured could maintain that the insurer had waived its right to contest a claim.

Subrogation

The coverage of a liability policy may induce an insurer to defend the insured in a lawsuit filed against him by a third party. Also the insurer can sue the third party in place of the insured if the said third party causes a loss covered by the policy held by the insured. This right is called subrogation and it is aimed at the party that is responsible for the loss, to bear the burden of the loss. This process also prevents an insured from recovering his losses twice, once each from the insurer and the responsible party.

However an insurer can subrogate claims only on certain specific policies. For instance, property and liability insurance policies allow subrogation because the basis for the payment of claims is indemnification or reimbursement of the insured for losses suffered.

But life insurance policies do not allow subrogation. In life insurance an insured is not indemnified for losses that could be measured in dollars because it is a policy for the insured and his nominee. A life insurance policy does not cover any liability to a third party.

It pays a fixed sum of money to the beneficiary and consequently the insured does not stand any chance of making two recoveries, from the insurer and the third party. As far as the insurer is concerned the question of suing a third party does not arise in the event of a claim.

Insurance Claim Management

Most insurance companies are identified by their efficiency in handling claims as it is one of the most important parts of the business if not the most important. It has been observed that the credit rating of many insurance companies took a beating due to poor claims handling. Many insurance companies in their stubbornness to dispute a claim had to take heavy losses after damaging litigation. But the best insurance companies take this aspect of their business seriously and have tried to improve their claims handling with more resources and technology.

LIMITATIONS ON RECOVERY

Business interruption policies typically provide that the insurer will be liable, within policy limits, for the insured's fixed charges and expenses necessarily continuing during the period following a total or partial suspension of business. Generally, however, coverage is provided only to the extent that income would have been earned if the contingency causing the suspension had not occurred.

Thus, it should be noted that the ISO Business Income Coverage Form, CP 0032 (1091), states in pertinent part:

Resumption of Operations

We will reduce the amount of your Business Income loss to the extent you can resume your "operations," in whole or in part, by using damaged or undamaged property (including merchandise or stock) at the described premises or elsewhere.

If you do not resume "operations," or do not resume "operations" as quickly as possible, we will pay based on the length of time it would have taken to resume "operations" as quickly as possible.

"EXPENSE" CONSTRUED

Under a business interruption policy, issues frequently arise regarding whether the construction of the term, "expense", under the policy. In A. Miller & Company v. Cincinnati Insurance Company, 577 N.E.2d 885 (Ill. App. Ct. 1991), the plaintiff contended that the term "expense", as used in the policy, included the cost of the raw material used to replace the inventory which the company used to prevent a loss of income. The Court held, however, that the term "expense" did not allow the insured to recover the costs of raw materials used to replenish his inventory since that would put the company in a better position than it would have been in if no breakdown had occurred.

Thus, the court concluded that allowing the raw material costs to be recovered under the policy would provide the insured with a double recovery. However, the court held that the term "expense" may include the costs for labor and utilities used in replacement of such inventory.

Also of interest is the case of Western America Inc. v. Aetna Casualty & Surety Company, 915 F.2d 1181 (8th Cir. 1990). In Western American, a fire destroyed most of Western America's adhesives manufacturing plant. Aetna insured Western and paid the losses for the plant and its contents. A dispute arose, however, over the interpretation of the policy's gross earnings and extra expenses clauses.

Aetna paid for the loss of gross earnings for 5 1/4 months of the suspension of business, but refused to pay for any extra expenses incurred to reduce losses during the rebuilding period. Western sued Aetna for lost rents, extra expenses and business interruption damages during the entire 10-month rebuilding period.

The jury awarded Western Rs.759,616, the full extent of its coverage under the gross earnings clause, but denied recovery for lost rents and extra expenses. Aetna argued that Western failed to prove profit and expense figures which were necessary to calculate the business interruption damages under the gross earnings clause.

In its analysis, the court considered a dispute involving a similar Aetna policy in Associated Photographers, Inc. v. Aetna Cas. & Sur. Co., 677 F.2d 1251 (8th Cir. 1988), and approved essentially the same jury instruction. Aetna claimed the instruction was misleading because it did not specifically instruct the jury to consider the theoretical time period it would have taken Western to rebuild, and because it directed the jury to add time to the business interruption period for delays caused by Aetna.

Tracking the wording of Aetna's policy, the district court charged the jury as follows with regard to the issue of damages for business interruption:

1. If your verdict is for Plaintiff Western Adhesives on its claim for loss of gross earnings due to business interruption, then, in determining Plaintiff Western Adhesive's damages under the Policy for Business Interruption (Gross Earnings) you should first determine from the evidence the length of the interruption period insured by the policy. If you determine from the evidence that there was a delay attributable to Defendant Aetna Casualty's failure to perform its duties under the policy, you may properly include that length of time in your calculation.
2. If you find Western Adhesives suffered a loss of gross earnings due to business interruption as a direct result of the fire, you should award Western Adhesives for the actual loss of earnings you believe it sustained as a direct result of the fire (business interruption) plus any expenses Plaintiff incurred in reducing its loss of earnings.
3. You are instructed that actual loss of earnings means the difference between the net profit you find Western Adhesives would have earned during the period of interruption and the net profit you find Western Adhesives did earn during the period of interruption.
4. If you find in favor of Plaintiff Western Adhesives, then you must determine the date on which the proof of loss for loss of gross earnings (business interruption) coverage was filed and award plaintiff Western Adhesives interest from that date at the rate of 9% per annum.

The appellate court agreed with the district court that there was sufficient evidence for the jury to determine the extra expenses which served to reduce the loss to Western's business due to the fire, and concluded that Aetna established no error in the district court's denial of its motion for a new trial.

Also, the appellate court held that the jury's verdict denying Western's extra expense claim was amply supported by the evidence. Thus, the judgment was affirmed.

"DEPRECIATION" CONSTRUED

Under a business interruption policy, issues frequently arise regarding whether an insured may include depreciation as an "expense" when the claimed business property has been totally destroyed.

The Court in Cohen Furniture Company v. St. Paul Insurance Company of Illinois, 573 N.E.2d 851, (Ill. App. Ct. 1991), held that an insured may not include depreciation as an "expense" under a business interruption policy where the business property has been totally destroyed, since depreciation only involves the useful life of an asset.

In Cohen, a dispute arose regarding the section of the business interruption policy which covered the "actual loss of earnings and extra expenses incurred because of necessary or potential interruption of business caused by covered direct damage to the building." An exclusion in the policy stated: "We won't include any charges and expenses which become unnecessary during the halt in your business."

The depreciation allowance represented the amount Cohen Furniture deducted on its income tax return for depreciation of the destroyed building and its improvements. In projecting loss of earnings under the business interruption policy, St. Paul subtracted from the earnings the "non-continuing expenses," i.e., expenses which were saved because the business was not in operation.

The appellate court held that St. Paul properly deducted the depreciation charge because an allowance for the depreciation can only be deducted during the useful life of an asset. Thus, a taxpayer cannot depreciate a non-existing asset. The court observed that once an asset has been destroyed, an insured cannot charge a depreciation expense.

It is important to note, however, that in Grevas v. United States Fidelity & Casualty Company, 604 N.E.2d 942 (Ill. 1992), the Illinois Supreme Court distinguished the appellate court's decision in Cohen.

In Grevas, the plaintiff owned an apartment building with coverage issued by USF&G. He suffered a loss by fire and applied to receive his net profits under the business interruption coverage. The amount was calculated by deducting the non-continuing expenses, such as utilities and lawn maintenance, from the building's gross income.

In addition, USF&G deducted an amount for depreciation of the premises, claiming that depreciation was an expense that was non-continuing. The trial court entered judgment for Grevas, finding that the policy was ambiguous as to whether depreciation was a non-continuing expense. The appellate court reversed and the plaintiff was granted leave to appeal.

The Supreme Court's distinction of Cohen and its reversal of the Appellate Court in the instant case was based upon a finding that, unlike the policy in Cohen, Grevas' policy contained coverage for both loss of gross earnings (a general clause), as well as, coverage for loss of rents (a specific clause). The Supreme Court further held that, in such cases, where both a general and a specific provision in a contract address the same subject, the more specific clause controls. Grevas at 944. Accordingly, the Supreme Court concluded that under the loss of rents provision, depreciation is solely a tax device and is not considered a noncontinuing charge or expense.

POLICY EXCLUSIONS AND LIMITATIONS

Most business interruption policies limit the insurer's liability to the extent that the business' charges and expenses would have been earned if the loss causing the interruption had not occurred. Partial business interruption limits the insurer's liability to a proportion of the liability that would have been incurred by a total suspension of business.

Further, the policy typically limits the period of recovery to the time required to repair, rebuild or replace the destroyed or damaged property with due diligence.

As noted previously, the insurer is generally liable for the "actual loss sustained" by the insured, resulting directly from necessary interruption of business, but not exceeding the reduction in gross earnings less charges and expenses which do not necessarily continue during the interruption of business.

For example, in Metalmasters of Minneapolis, Inc. v. Liberty Mutual Insurance Company, 461 N.W.2d 496 (Minn. Ct. App. 1990), the appellate court upheld the trial court's determination that Metalmasters incurred no "actual loss" in sales since Metalmasters presented no evidence of lost sales and proved no reduction in gross earnings.

The appellate court further agreed with the trial court that, without a proven actual loss, the business interruption coverage did not extend to the value of services provided by Metalmasters' president, in the amount of Rs.60,000, which were used on cleanup during the interruption of business rather than to the advantage of the corporation.

AMBIGUOUS EXCLUSION LANGUAGE

An insurer may not usually rely on the definition section of a policy to define ambiguous terms which are used in the exclusion section of the policy to the extent that such an application of terms would preclude coverage in almost any situation.

For example, in Pressman v. Aetna Cas. & Sur. Co., 574 A.2d 757 (R.I. 1990), the plaintiff, a clinical psychologist, lost business because of a power failure when a tree adjacent to his property fell onto the power line that ran to his building. Because of the power outage, he was forced to cancel appointments with all of his scheduled patients, and he was unable to perform computerized diagnostic testing.

In addition, after the electrical power was restored, one of his two computers was not functioning. Pressman's business owner's insurer, Aetna Casualty, refused to reimburse him for his economic loss, claiming that coverage was excluded since the interruption of power took place away from the described premises. The trial court granted summary judgment in favor of Aetna.

On appeal, the appellate court determined that no issue of material fact existed, since no one contradicted the fact that the loss of power occurred when a tree collapsed on land adjacent to the property of the insured, severing the power line. It held that in construing the phase "away from the described premises", the trial judge had relied upon a definition of the term "premises" applicable to a different section in the policy.

To apply the special definition from another section to the exclusion section would preclude coverage in almost any circumstance, unless the insured had his own generator located inside the building, which, the court believed, would be unconscionable.

Thus, since it was not unreasonable for Pressman to have believed that his loss would be covered in these circumstances, the judgment was vacated, and the case remanded for trial on the merits.

ENFORCEMENT OF ORDINANCE EXCLUSION

In Cohen Furniture Company v. St. Paul Ins. Co. of Illinois, 573 N.E.2d 851, (Ill. App. Ct. 1991), a fire destroyed the plaintiff's building, which had been built in 1971 and did not contain a fire suppression system. In 1978, the city's building code was amended to require the installation of fire suppression systems in the construction of all new buildings.

Following the loss, Cohen Furniture replaced the old store with a new building which included a Rs.54,000 fire suppression system. However, the policy excluded losses caused directly or indirectly by the enforcement of any law governing the use, construction, repair or demolition of buildings.

The Illinois Appellate Court held that where an exclusion clause precludes coverage for losses directly or indirectly caused by the enforcement of an ordinance, the trial court should have granted summary judgement to the insurer where the insured rebuilt his building with a fire suppression system required by law, since the installation of such a system was a direct result of an ordinance and within the express terms of the exclusion.

Note: Other building loss exclusion cases cited by the court included Hertog v. Milwaukee Mutual Insurance Co. (1987) 415 N.W.2d 370; Stahlberg v. Travelers Indemnity Co. (1978) 568 S.W.2d 79; Unified School District No. 285 v. St. Paul Fire and Marine Insurance Co. (1981) 6 Kan.App.2d 244, 627 P.2d 1147; Hewins et al. v. London Assurance Corp. (1903) 184 Mass. 177, 68 NE 62. Hewins holds that the insurer is not liable for costs attributable to building law requirements, and is the most widely cited case upholding business laws exclusions.

It is interesting to note a contrary holding in the case of Linnton Plywood Assoc. v. Protection Mutual Ins. Co., 760 F.Supp. 170 (D. Or. 1991). In Linnton, the plaintiff prevailed in an action for business interruption by presenting evidence that its decision to suspend operations at the mill, in the absence of an adequate fire protection system, was consistent with its duty under the policy not to increase a hazard.

PRACTICAL CONSIDERATIONS

Confronted with an insured business interruption loss, risk managers should follow a nine-point plan, a broker advises.

Brian O'Neil, assistant vice-president in the claim department of Frank B. Hall of California, reviewed these points during a workshop at the second Asia-Pacific Risk Management Conference co-sponsored by the Risk & Insurance Management Society Inc. and the Risk & Insurance Management Association of Singapore (copyright 1990 Crain Communications, Inc., Business Insurance, 11/12/90):

1. Call the broker or agent, who needs to involve the insurer immediately;
2. Make decisions in the company's best interest, regardless of whether they fit into insurance coverage;
3. Assign an account number to the loss so that all costs can be captured;
4. Provide the insurer with access to the people that know the impact of the loss and what needs to be done to restore operations;

5. Determine the potential loss of sales, which the insurer will need to estimate loss reserves;
6. Identify the extra expenses that could reduce the loss of sales. These could include the cost of continuing production at the current site, moving to a temporary location, using other company facilities, contracting out work and paying overtime and bonuses;
7. Evaluate what must be done to get back into business, either at the current location or a temporary location. Also, determine what products are most important to get back into production and identify the extra expenses already being incurred;
8. Gather all documents to submit the business interruption claim;
9. Continue to provide all necessary and relevant documentation to the insurer.

DEFINITION AND EXTENT OF LIFE INSURANCE

Mankind is exposed to many serious hazards such as fire, disability and premature death, the happening of which, from the standpoint of the individual, it is impossible to foretell or prevent, but the effects of which, such as the loss of property or earnings, it is highly important to provide against. It is the function of insurance in its numerous forms to enable individuals to safeguard themselves against such misfortunes by having the losses of the unfortunate few paid by the contributions of the many who are exposed to the same risk. If the hazard under consideration is that of premature death, the loss suffered is indemnified through life insurance. From the community standpoint life insurance may be defined as "that social device for making accumulations to meet uncertain losses through premature death which is carried out through the transfer of the risks of many individuals to one person or a group of persons". From the standpoint of the individual, however, life insurance, may be defined as consisting of a contract, whereby for a stipulated compensation, called the premium, one party (the insurer) agrees to pay the other (the insured), or his beneficiary, a fixed sum upon the happening of death or some other specified event.

Life insurance had its origin in history much later than the leading forms of property insurance and its real rise to importance dates back only about half a century. The first attempts at associated life insurance, as far as is known, were undertaken in Great Britain. In 1699 there was formed the "Society of Assurance for Widows and Orphans" and in 1706 "The Amicable Society for a Perpetual Assurance Office". It has been estimated that between 1699 and 1720 probably fifty life-insurance schemes were started in Great Britain but all were conducted under methods very defective as compared with those now in general use; in fact, Mr. Holcombe concludes: "It may be taken as established that no plan of life insurance as we now understand it had been contemplated by any company or society, or had been considered by any legislature in Europe prior to the year 1760". In 1762, when the total amount of life insurance in Great Britain is said not to have exceeded Rs.350,000, the Equitable Assurance Society of London commenced operations, and this society may be regarded as the first to use the modern system of insurance, its policies being issued for fixed amounts and the premiums graded according to age.

But while the institution of life insurance was first carefully studied and applied in Great Britain, its greatest growth has been in the United States, dating chiefly since the Civil War. A few figures will make clear the extent and rapidity of this development. Exclusive of annuity contracts, it has been estimated that the total number of life-insurance policies in the United States at the beginning of the nineteenth century did not exceed one hundred. By 1860 the companies reporting to the Insurance Department of the State of New York showed a total of only 56,000 policies with a face value of Rs.163,000,000, while the annual premium income amounted to only Rs.4,700,000 and the assets to Rs.24,000,000. By 1870 the companies authorized to do business in the state of New York showed the following totals: Annual premium income,

Rs.90,000,000; number of policies, 740,000; face value of insurance, Rs.2,000,000,000; and assets Rs.270,000,000. During the next decade the companies experienced a decline, but following 1880 the business enjoyed a phenomenal and almost uninterrupted growth.

It is possible to present only approximately the total insurance carried by the numerous corporations and associations now operating in the United States. Some idea, however, of the present magnitude of the life-insurance business in the United States may be obtained from the aggregates for the year 1913, published in the Insurance Year Book. At the close of that year, it appears that as regards 259 companies the amount of insurance in force aggregated Rs.20,564,000,000, the annual premium income Rs.715,000,000 and the total income Rs.925,000,000, the annual payments to policyholders Rs.468,000,000, and the admitted assets Rs.4,658,000,000. To these enormous totals, however, it is necessary to add the business of the numerous fraternal orders which grant insurance. At the close of 1913, 509 such orders carried certificates aggregating Rs.9,622,000,000 while their annual income amounted to Rs.144,000,000, their annual claims to Rs.101,000,000, and their assets to Rs.183,000,000. The vastness of these figures can scarcely be comprehended. They testify to the fact that the value of life-insurance protection is rapidly being recognized by the rank and file of the nation's population. At present over 32,000,000 policies and fraternal certificates, aggregating over Rs.30,000,000,000 of insurance, are carried in the United States, and over Rs.569,000,000 is distributed annually in claims; yet these enormous figures are small compared with what they will be at the close of the next generation.

COMBINATION OF MANY RISKS INTO A GROUP IS NECESSARY TO MAKE THE LAW OF AVERAGE APPLY

Our definition of life insurance, it will be recalled, involved "the transfer of risks of many individuals to one person or a group of persons". Such a combination of risks is absolutely essential if the business is to be established on a basis other than speculation or gambling. To eliminate the speculative factor it is necessary to proceed on the theory that the larger the number of separate risks of a like nature combined into one group, the less uncertainty will there be as to the amount of loss that will be incurred.

To insure a single life for Rs.1,000 during a given year, it is clear, is in the nature of a gamble, because the individual must either die or survive that period, with the result that there is either a 100 percent, loss or gain. If the number of persons insured is increased to one hundred the element of uncertainty will still be present to a large extent, although the variations in the number dying or surviving the year will be much less than that noted in the preceding case. But if 500,000 lives of similar physical condition are combined in the same group, and more than that number of lives are now insured in each of several American companies, the fluctuation in the rate of death from year to year will vary only by the smallest fraction of 1 percent, with the result that the company will be able to determine in advance the amount of its death claims and thus to place its business upon a non-speculative basis. In fact, if the number of lives insured by a company were so large as to make the application of the law of average perfect, practically all uncertainty as to the amount of loss that would be experienced during a given period would be removed. As has been well said:

When the insurance is furnished by a company with capital or surplus which answers as a given guarantee of stability, it becomes a business, instead of a speculation, the distinction being that while an individual who assumes a single risk either loses or gains thereby the whole amount involved, the company which takes many, by means of the aggregate business reduces the possible variations to narrow limits and really makes of insurance a business attended with less peril than almost any other.... During a given year an individual either dies or he survives the year; the result is a 100 percent loss or a 100 percent gain, if one wagers upon the one life. But make one hundred thousand of these bets upon persons of the same age and like physical condition and the variation in the result will not be 2 percent, usually, instead of 200 percent. There is nothing more uncertain than life and nothing more certain than life insurance.

NECESSITY OF ACCUMULATING A FUND FOR THE PAYMENT OF CLAIMS

While all forms of insurance are alike in that they require for their successful operation a combination of many risks into a group, they are vitally different as regards the nature of the risks covered. In this respect the chief difference between life and other forms of insurance is that in the latter the contingency insured against may or may not happen, and as regards the great majority of policies written, does not happen while in life insurance the event against which protection is granted, namely death, is a "hazard converging into certainty". It is necessary, therefore, if a life insurance policy is to protect the insured during the whole of life, to provide not only against the risk of death each year, but also to accumulate an adequate fund for the purpose, as Mr. Dawson states, "of meeting at the ultimate limit of human life an absolutely certain claim if one has up to that time been escaped". He further adds: "It was failure to see the necessity for providing for an increasing hazard, converging into certainty, which has caused many serious errors in the fundamental plans of some institutions formed to furnish life insurance, and the thing which separates plans of insurance into sound and unsound is precisely whether intelligent regard for this principle has guided the company in determining its rates of premium and the management and disposition of its funds".

NECESSITY OF ACCUMULATING THIS FUND ACCORDING TO SCIENTIFIC PRINCIPLES AND A WORKABLE METHOD

In accumulating the fund referred to in the preceding section it is important for the companies to take into account several other characteristics which differentiate life insurance from other forms of insurance. In the first place, the persons combining for life insurance are not of the same age, and it is

1913 the reserve value of the policies in force in the 259 American legal-reserve companies, reported in the Insurance Year Book, amounted to Rs.3,903,000,000 or nearly 84 percent, of their total admitted assets.

LIFE INSURANCE CHANGES UNCERTAINTY INTO CERTAINTY AND IS THE OPPOSITE OF GAMBLING

Although life insurance serves indirectly to increase the productivity of the community by eliminating worry and increasing initiative, its direct economic function is to change uncertainty into certainty and thus enable the insured to transfer the hazard of premature death to the insurer at the lowest possible cost. The real gain from life insurance is due to the combination of many separate risks into a group with a view to making possible the "substitution of certain for uncertain loss". As already explained, the larger the number of separate risks comprising a group, the less uncertainty will there be as to the amount of loss, and the less the uncertainty of loss the smaller will be the premium that the company needs to collect annually from the insured.

This function of insurance is perhaps most readily understood in connection with fire insurance. Thus let us assume that each of 5,000 persons owns a house valued at Rs.10,000, that all the houses are alike, and that the annual loss by fire as regards the entire number, although varying slightly from year to year, averages one-half of 1 percent, of the value, or Rs.50. In the absence of any system of insurance making possible the application of the law of average, it is clear that none of these owners can effect any arrangement which will place them in a position of absolute security. At best they can only anticipate their uncertain losses by practicing self-insurance, i.e. by increasing their rentals by an amount considerably in excess of the average annual loss of Rs.50. But even assuming that they can increase their rentals by four or five times the amount actually necessary under a system of insurance, they will still remain subject to a large gamble. At the end of the year the great majority of these owners, since they suffer no loss, would have the entire extra sum collected from tenants as a clear gain, while as regards those unfortunate few who suffer a total loss the extra sum collected would prove woefully inadequate to indemnify the value destroyed.

But let us now assume that these 5,000 house-owners can combine their risks into a group. By doing this they can substitute for the great uncertainty of loss which confronted them as individuals a certain definitely known loss, amounting on the average to Rs.50 per house and Rs.250,000 for the group. This sum plus a proper addition for expenses, contingencies and reasonable profit, is all that the company needs to charge in order absolutely to secure these owners against the risk of loss by fire". The risk that an insurance company carries is far less than the sum of the risks of the insured, and as the size of the company increases the disproportion becomes greater". Now just as each house-owner was enabled to use fire insurance to substitute certainty for uncertainty at the lowest possible cost, so it is also possible through life insurance to hedge against the uncertainty of life by providing for the payment of a definite sum of money at death, whenever that may occur, to replace the economic value of the deceased individual. From a family and business standpoint nearly all lives possess an economic value which may at any time be snuffed out by death, and it is as reasonable to insure against the loss of this value as it is to protect oneself against the loss of property. In the absence of insurance we saw that property-owners could at best practice only some form of self-insurance, and that it was impossible for them to effect any arrangement which would give absolute certainty.

Similarly, in the absence of a system of life insurance which makes possible the application of the law of average, no arrangement can be found which will render certain the indemnification of the value of a human life lost through death. The practice of saving such a sum in anticipation of probable death by no means takes the place of insurance as an agency in substituting certainty for uncertainty. because saving requires time and death may occur before the savings fund has reached an appreciable size. Unlike the practice of saving a life-insurance policy means certainty because it guarantees a definite escate from the moment the first premium is paid. Moreover, it furnishes this element of certainty to the public at the lowest possible cost since the companies are enabled through the combination of many risks to determine the exact average cost of the protection for the entire group. From the company's point of view we have seen that life insurance is essentially non-speculative; in fact, probably no other business operates with greater certainty. But it is equally important to remember that from the insured point of view life insurance is also the antithesis of gambling. Nothing is more uncertain than life, and life insurance offers the only sure method of changing that uncertainty into certainty. Failure of the head of a family to insure his life against the sudden loss of his value through death amounts to gambling with the greatest of all chances, and the gamble is a particularly mean-one since in case of loss the dependent family and not the gambler must suffer the consequences.

BACKGROUND

Commercial property insurance claims frequently involve more than a mere loss of tangible business property. Economic damages in the form of loss of income from suspended operations, or from extra expenses suffered as a result of the loss are also typically sought by business owners. This article will examine the fundamental aspects of business interruption and extra-expense insurance coverages, and will provide an overview of several related cases.

SCOPE OF COVERAGE

Business interruption insurance is designed to protect the prospective earnings of the insured business. It is also designed to do for the insured, in the event of a loss, what the business would have done for itself if an interruption in the operation of the business had not occurred. Thus, business interruption insurance is designed to indemnify the insured-business against losses arising from its inability to continue the normal operations and functions of the business. Coverage is triggered by the total or partial suspension of business operations due to the loss, loss of use, or damage to all or part of the buildings, plant, machinery, equipment, or other personal property thereof, as the result of a covered cause of loss.

Coverage is generally provided for the "period of restoration", which is usually considered to be the period which would be required to rebuild, repair or replace the damaged property at the described premises with reasonable speed and similar quality. It usually commences with the date of such damage or destruction and it is not usually limited by the date of expiration of the policy.

Business interruption coverage is generally provided by a rider or endorsement to a commercial property insurance policy. The coverage typically provides that the insurer is not liable except for losses caused directly by a covered cause of loss, i.e., a hazard or peril insured against as a matter of contract. Moreover, actual profits and business expenses covered by the policy are usually determined in a manner which gives due consideration for the character of the business along with the manner in which it conducts its business activities.

INSURED'S DUTIES IN THE EVENT OF LOSS

Under the Insurance Services Office (ISO) Business Income Coverage Form, CP 0032 1091 (1990), a policy which is adopted by many insurers, the insured must see that the following are done in the event of a covered loss:

1. Notify the police if a law may have been broken.
2. Give prompt notice of the direct physical loss or damage. Include a description of the property involved.
3. As soon as possible, give a description of how, when, and where the direct physical loss or damage occurred.
4. Take all reasonable steps to protect the Covered Property from further damage by a Covered Cause of Loss. If feasible, set the damaged property aside and in the best possible order for examination. Also keep a record of

expenses for emergency and temporary repairs for consideration in the settlement of the claim. This will not increase the Limit of Insurance.

5. As often as may be reasonably required, permit inspection of the property proving the loss or damage and allow examination of books and records. Also permit to be taken samples of damaged and undamaged property for inspection, testing and analysis, and permit copies from books and records.
6. Send a signed and sworn proof of loss containing the information requested to investigate the claim. You must do this within 60 days after request. We will supply you with the necessary forms.
7. Cooperate with the investigation or settlement of the claim.
8. If you intend to continue your business, you must resume all or part of your "operations" as quickly as possible.

DUTIES IMPOSED UNDER THE NOTICE PROVISION

It is important to note at this point that the duties imposed under the notice provision (i.e., "[g]ive prompt notice of the direct physical loss or damage") are not to be considered as technical requirements merely for the convenience of the insurer, but rather are valid perquisites for coverage. Mitchell Buick & Oldsmobile Sales, Inc. v. National Dealer Services, Inc., 485 N.E.2d 1281 (Ill. App. Ct. 1985).

Many policy provisions which establish when an insured must notify its insurer concerning covered occurrences also require notification "within a reasonable time", considering all relevant facts and circumstances. When the material facts are undisputed, an insured's diligence in forwarding its notice to the insurer becomes solely a question of law. Grasso v. Mid-Century Ins. Co., 536 N.E.2d 977 (Ill. App. Ct. 1989).

Among the factors to be considered in determining if an insured has acted within a reasonable time in giving notice are: (1) the presence or absence of the insured's sophistication in the world of commerce and insurance; (2) awareness on the part of the insured that an occurrence as defined by the policy has taken place; and (3) once aware of an occurrence, the diligence with which the insured ascertains whether policy coverage is available. American Family Mutual Insurance Company v. Blackburn, 566 N.E.2d 889 (Ill. App. Ct. 1991); appeal denied, 575 N.E.2d 911 (Ill. 1991).

It should be noted, however, that under Illinois law, if the insurer receives timely notice of the occurrence from a third party, this actual notice may satisfy the policy requirement for the insured to give notice to its insurer. Casualty Indem. Exchange v. Village of Crete, 731 F.2d 457 (7th Cir. 1984).

NECESSITY OF PROOF OF LOSS

As noted above, many current policies require that the insured submit a signed sworn proof of loss within 60 days of the insurer's request. Many other policies demand that the proof be submitted within 60 days of the date of loss, even if the insurer does not otherwise request the form. Needless to say, the period within which the proof can be filed can be waived or extended by the insurer. It is interesting to note that in Gregory v. Continental Insurance Company, 575 So. 2d 534 (Miss. 1990), no proof of loss was submitted by the plaintiff prior to the filing of suit, and no written demand for payment was ever made on Continental. Subsequent to the filing of the suit, however, the plaintiff submitted the required documents and sought recovery under the terms of the policy.

The Court held that, although an insurer's duty to promptly pay a legitimate claim does not end because a lawsuit has been filed against it for nonpayment, Continental was not required under its contract to make any payment unless and until the proof of loss provisions of the policy were satisfied. Moreover, the Court concluded that the insured was not entitled to punitive damages where the terms of the policy obligated the insured to submit a proof of loss as a condition precedent to recovery, and where the insured had failed to do so. It is important to note that the refusal of a corporation's officials to give information to their insurer in response to interrogatories, whether under advice of counsel or not, may be deemed to be a breach of the policy provision which requires an insured to submit to an examination under oath. Gipps Brewing Corp. v. Central Mfrs' Mut. Ins. Co., 147 F.2d 6 (7th Cir. 1945). Moreover, under Illinois law, fraud and false swearing is ordinarily a question of fact for the jury, but it becomes a question of law if the concealments or misrepresentations by an insured cannot in any way be seen as innocent. Lykos v. American Home Ins. Co., 609 F.2d 314 (7th Cir. 1979).

AUTO INSURANCE

Auto Insurance or Automobile Insurance (also known as Vehicle Insurance, Motor Insurance, or Car Insurance) refers to the insurance which can be bought for trucks, cars, and other types of vehicles. The principal objective of an Auto Insurance Policy is to offer safeguards against adverse financial consequences resulting from motor vehicle accidents (MVAs). The Automobile Insurance Company has the discretion to adjudge that a car is wholly destructed (write-off or totaled) if it seems that the replacement cost would be lower compared to repairing costs.

In case of Auto Insurance, coverage is available for some or all the parties given below:

- The party insured
- The insured car
- Third parties In a large number of countries, buying Auto Insurance is mandatory to drive on public or state highways.

The basis of charging the premium is dependent on the following factors: the coverage, the age, gender, and driving history of the driver, and the distance covered by the car.

The different types of coverage that are available in Automobile Insurance include the following:

- Liability Coverage (Combined Single Limit & Split Limits)

- Collision Coverage
- Comprehensive Coverage
- Loss of Use Coverage
- Underinsured/Uninsured Coverage
- Loan/Lease Payoff Coverage (GAP Coverage or GAP Insurance)
- Car Towing Insurance (Roadside Assistance Coverage)

LIFE INSURANCE COUNCIL OF INDIA

Structure

- The Life Insurance Council will have an Executive Committee of 21 members of which 2 will be from the IRDA and the rest from licensed life insurers
- The Committee will set up standards of conduct and practices for efficient customer service, advise IRDA on controlling insurers' expenses and serve as a forum that helps maintain healthy market conduct
- It will create and manage a process for agent examination and certification
- The Life Insurance Council is funded by the Life Insurers in India

The Purpose

- The Life Insurance Council seeks to play a significant and complementary role in transforming India's life insurance industry into a vibrant, trustworthy and profitable service, helping the people of India on their journey to prosperity.

Its Mission

- To function as an active forum to aid, advise and assist insurers in maintaining high standards of conduct and service to policyholders
- Advise the supervisory authority in the matter of controlling expenses

- Interact with the Government and other bodies on policy matters
- Actively participate in spreading insurance awareness in India
- Take steps to develop education and research insurance
- Help bring to India the benefit of the best practices in the world

The Council Will

- Strive for a positive image of the industry through media, forums and opinion- makers and enhance consumer confidence in the industry
- Assist the industry in maintaining high standards of ethics and governance
- Promote awareness regarding the role and benefits of life insurance
- Organize structured, regular and proactive discussions with Government, lawmakers and Regulators on matters relevant to the contribution by the life insurance industry and act as an effective liaison between them
- Conduct research on operational, economic, legislative, regulatory and customer-oriented issues in life insurance, publish monographs on current developments in life insurance and contribute to the development of the sector
- Set up the Mortality and Morbidity Information Bureau (MMIB) and take an active role in its functioning
- Set up similar organizations for the benefit of the life insurance industry
- Act as a forum of interaction with organizations in other segments of the financial services sector
- Play a leading role in insurance education, research, training, discussion forums and conferences

- Provide help and guidance to members when necessary
- Be an active link between the Indian life insurance industry and the global markets

Legislations & Control

- Address common issues in legislation and practice. Interface with the various other regulatory bodies on behalf of the insurance industry.
- Identify regularly the important issues to be taken up with Government and/or IRDA & PFRDA and make presentations on behalf of the industry
- Prepare benchmarks for the industry in all areas of operation and help maintain high standards of conduct, ethics and governance
- Take measures to prevent practices that are detrimental to the interests of the policyholders

Training & Certification

- Take up the work relating to the training, examination and certification of Agents as provided in the Insurance Act
- Play a positive role in establishing standards, training of officials and intermediaries not only in products and sales but also other aspects relevant to the life insurance industry and lift the level of professionalism
- Conduct professional development programs in collaboration with international councils and life insurance institutes

Education & Awareness

- Launch regular insurance awareness programs
- Facilitate the conducting of Continuous Development Programs for intermediaries
- Provide structured regular information to the public about the industry

- Launch an interactive website/Life Insurance Journals/ newsletters
- Organise / participate in major conferences, seminars, workshops and lectures by Indian/visiting experts on insurance and related areas
- Facilitate knowledge-exchange programs (both in India and with Councils abroad) to develop and upgrade the skills of local insurance professionals
- Co-ordinate with educational institutions in India and overseas to encourage research, professional development courses etc.
- Elevate the profession of insurance selling and that of the Advisor, to that of financial analysts and planners through certification programs developed in conjunction with Indian and International institutions.

BIBLIOGRAPHY

Arrow, Kenneth J.: *Social Choice and Individual Values,* New York, Wiley, 1951.

Campbell, J.Y., Lo, A.W.: *The Econometrics of Financial Markets,* Princeton University Press, 1996.

Chaudhuri, Pramit: *The Indian Economy: Poverty and Development,* New York, St. Martin's Press, 1979.

Dhingra, C.: *The Indian Economy: Resources, Planning, Development, and Problems,* Delhi, Sultan Chand, 1983.

Greer, Douglas F.: *Industrial Organization and Public Policy,* MacMillan Publishing Company, 1992.

Ishwar, C.: *The Indian Economy: Resources, Planning, Development, and Problems,* Delhi, Sultan Chand, 1983.

Little, I.M.D.: *India: Macroeconomics and Political Economy, 1964-1991,* Washington, World Bank, 1994.

Mongia, J.N.: *India's Economic Development Strategies, 1951-2000 A.D.*. New Delhi, Allied, 1986.

Pranab, K.: *The Political Economy of Development in India,* Delhi, Oxford University Press, 1984.

Sargent, Thomas J.: *Dynamic Macroeconomic Theory,* Harvard University Press, 1987.

Tirole, Jean: *The Theory of Industrial Organization,* MIT Press, 1988.

Williamson, Jeffrey G.: *American Inequality: A Macroeconomic History,* New York, Academic Press, 1980.

Xavier Sala-i-Martin: *Economic Growth.* McGraw-Hill, 1995.

INDEX

O

P

R

S

T

W

□□□